Fine That

~ *an Orkney Island life*

Written by
Julia Welstead

Illustrated by
Moonart

Treb Publishing

Contents

~

For my gorgeous boys ~ Miles, Dale, Fenning & Nic

Foreword

Three years ago I was standing at the school gates on one of those bitingly cold Edinburgh days, waiting for the bell to shrill and for my wee boys to come running out to me. To distract myself from the icy chill running up my spine I got chatting to the woman next to me. I prattled on about my dreams of islands and beaches, animals and land, space and freedom. As the bell rang she looked me in the eye and said "you should write" - a somewhat enigmatic statement, but I went home and did just that.

Now I'm on a wee island in Orkney, living the dream of that day and loving every minute of it. But the biggest surprise to me is that, having started writing I've never stopped. Writing has become a part of my life and I love it. Every week I write a column for the Weekend section of "The Scotsman". This book is the accumulation of those articles to date, beautifully embellished by Moonart, who have captured the essence of this island so astutely.

How can I begin to acknowledge everyone who has helped me with this book which is, after all, about my life? From my parents for bearing me to my children for bearing with me it's an impossible task to mention all those who have touched my life. The essential protagonists without whom this book would not exist are:
Maggie O'Kane for prompting me to write.
The Scotsman for publishing my words and therefore keeping the wolf from my door.
Ian, Irene and Liz Brown for proof reading the book.
Many folk in Orkney for their help, advice and generosity.
Miles, Dale and Fenning for being with me through thick and thin.
Best buddy Nic, for arriving out of the blue and bettering absolutely everything.

Read on. I hope you enjoy my journey.

Migrating North

~ *Spring & Summer*
2001

Why & Where
~ *February*

"I'm going to be sick very soon."

We're driving north on the A9, somewhere between Inverness and Golspie, when I hear those dreaded words.

Luckily, my five-year-old is a very organised person who can inform me of such impending events in a calm, logical manner. "Soon" means we can make it to the next lay-by. "Very soon" involves the hard shoulder and flashing lights. He never says "now" – for obvious reasons.

I suppose Dale's expert ability to gauge the timing of these unfortunate incidents stems from the fact that he has done a lot of travelling, especially since I split up with the father of my three sons and we left the Hebrides for some city life in Edinburgh.

I chose this city as a temporary refuge because I know and love it so well from my childhood and student days. I was born and brought up here in the 1960's, returned to train as a nurse in 1979 and returned once more in 1999 to seek refuge from a failed relationship. Perhaps Edinburgh is my geographical security blanket. My comfort zone.

It will certainly always be my favourite city, for its wide cobbled streets, its imposing, sombre architecture, its mature, lush gardens and quite simply because it is so familiar to me. In these last two years Edinburgh has been a good home for us. We have had some fun and healed some wounds.

But despite having been born here, I am not a natural city dweller. Cities hold a limited appeal for me. I am not very good at coping with small spaces and lots of people. I begin to feel claustrophobic and in need of more elbowroom and air. My favourite places (Australia, Southern Morocco and West Scotland spring to mind) all have vast acres of nothingness and huge skies.

Most of all I hate the lack of freedom and the constant need to be security minded. In the last two years I have locked myself out of our town house four times. Getting back in has respectively involved: a locksmith; a fire engine with eight strapping lads (one to climb the ladder and seven to stand around looking hunky) and two agile friends both of whom managed to climb up to my first floor kitchen window.

On many other occasions I have left the front door unlocked or even wide open. The car is never locked. Please don't tell my insurers. I'm hopeless at parking into anything less than a coach-sized space. Traffic terrifies me. Most of all, there's no room to keep animals and to grow food and nowhere for the children to run free.

With thoughts like these it is definitely time to move out of the city. Time to find a place where my children can grow up with space and beauty and the freedom to explore it. A place with a small but thriving community and a good school. A place where I can afford to buy a property large enough to have dogs, ponies and hens and a garden full of vegetables.

A very personal desire has always been to live with sea and sand close by (friends call me a northern beach bum). I do so love to find sand in children's ears and trouser pockets and socks.

I began my search in central Scotland and looked further and further north in an effort to find something that met my list of criteria. When even Caithness didn't feel right I realised that the island life had got into my blood and I should be searching beyond the confines of mainland Scotland.

So we are heading up the A9 to Orkney for a week of house viewing. It is mid-February with snow in the air and we have a very geriatric (wish I could say vintage) car: is this such a good plan?

Why am I thinking of moving to a remote archipelago chillingly close to the Arctic Circle? (And why on Earth am I bringing my three and five year old boys on a househunting trip with me? Well, they were all set to visit their father. Unfortunately he had a last minute crisis and just had to dash off on holiday to Mexico with his latest girlfriend. No no, really, there is no hint of bitterness in my words.)

Miles (nine going on 30) has accepted a better offer, to stay with a friend in Drumnadrochit. Sledging, swimming in Inverness, late nights and James Bond movies seem to have been the main lures. So we part company and Fenning (my three-year-old (male) drama queen), Dale and I head north.

Undaunted by my own utter madness, we whizz through the snowy wastes of Sutherland and Caithness and arrive, breathless with the buzz of a miracle experienced (the car made it!) at the breezy, but not at all balmy, port of Scrabster.

We face a two-hour crossing to Stromness, over the notoriously lumpen waters of the Pentland Firth. Dale is sick out on deck before we have even left Scrabster. Hmmm....

Have you ever been to Orkney? This crossing, Scrabster to Stromness, has to be amongst the most stunning in the world. The ferry follows the sandstone cliffs of the West Coast of Hoy and passes impressively close to the Old Man of Hoy, a fantastic 450-foot sea stack. The pump of adrenaline that surged through my body when I first saw this put paid to any queasiness in an instant.

Our five days in Orkney pass in a whirl of houses to see, schools to be shown around, ferries to outlying islands and evenings with my friends who live there. The boys develop fast-flow colds and hacking coughs. I administer sticky syrup concoctions, mop noses and proffer juice.

The only plus about this dismal turn of events is that they are quite content to slumber in the back of the car, each wrapped in one of my "sheep" (excessively large woolly jumpers of the sort seldom seen since the advent of the much more practical "fleecy") while we trundle around the Orcadian roads. The usual boy-child demands for attention, action and entertainment are temporarily subdued. And for small men, they are really being rather well behaved patients.

The stack of house schedules by my side dwindles and I haven't yet found a house that warms my heart. On our last sleet-driven afternoon I negotiate a pot-holed, flooded track to view a cottage with plenty of "potential" only to find that I cannot gain access. Frustrated, I drift on and turn instinctively off the road at the welcoming sight of smoke billowing from the chimney of a friendly wee farmhouse.

This track ends in a yard facing a stretch of stone-built byres and overlooking a sheltered garden. The appearance of a woman at the farmhouse door makes me uncomfortably aware that I have trespassed. Embarrassed, I explain that I am house hunting and strayed up here because this place looked so invitingly cosy. By remarkable chance (fate?) it turns out that this property is probably coming up for sale soon! Wow, how did I manage that?

So I have found my idyll. An old, cosy (as in four foot thick walls and small, deep-set windows) house set in herb rich pastures (yes, I can tell this even though it's February – my Biology degree has not gone entirely to waste) with a workshop, a stable and a path leading to the beach. I cannot imagine anywhere I would rather live. Now I am keen to get home and work out how I can possibly buy this place.

~

How
~ March

Back down south to the Stockbridge Colonies of Edinburgh and it's the Sunday before school restarts. Miles arrives back from his friend's. They fell out mid-way through the week but luckily the erstwhile friend has a younger sister who happily played dens, sledging and tree climbing with Miles.

Dale and Fenning are running wild and naked (well, I wanted to get all their clothes washed and anyway they love the freedom and I'm sure it's good for their souls) around the house being goodies and baddies and dead then reincarnated as some other, yet more powerful, being. I thought I was bringing them up to be pacifists, but hey...

Sunday night. I can barely keep my eyes open as I allocate crisps, apples and mini fruit juice cartons to three packed-lunch boxes (sandwiches to be added in the morning) and dig out the relevant school uniforms from the pile of clean laundry. As usual, I wish for colour-coded socks as I rake the pile for something that might match in both design and size.

This week I have travelled several hundred miles of road and some of sea. I have looked after two sickly children and run the gauntlet of a traditional Scottish B&B (white slice, constant background TV and crocheted loo roll covers are still alive and kicking). I have searched for, and found, my ideal home and I have re-thought my life over and over. It's time for bed.

~

What to wear? What to wear?

"Mum! It's time to go!"

School mornings are extremely regimented for us. Dale gets up first and plays cars with increasing volume until Miles and I surface. Fruit, toast, yoghurt, last night's rice pudding – anything really – get consumed ferociously by Dale, reluctantly by Miles.

Flapjacks are our latest breakfast idea: my earth-mother response to the big cereal companies marketing their products in handy snack bar form as a supposedly healthy option. I drink very weak Lapsang Souchong tea and feel slightly nauseous. Surely too much wine and too little sleep wouldn't have anything to do with it?

We all get dressed and try to remember to brush our teeth and wipe the jam from our mouths. Finally there is Fenning – the only three year old I know of who just can't seem to make it out of bed in the mornings (isn't that supposed to be a teenage thing?). I sort of pour Fenning into his clothes, place a flapjack in one of his hands and piggy-back or buggy him to nursery. He is usually awake by the time we get there.

All of this is fine as long as I don't care what I look like. I mean, I pretty much always manage to put something on (although I admit that the pyjamas have made it to the school gates on occasion) but glamour is not a priority. This morning is a different matter. I'm on the hunt for a mortgage.

I am a single parent. I have been self-employed for a mere 6 months before which I was a full-time Mum (which some joker has decreed is a form of unemployment). My accounts show that the business has plenty of room for growth.... Would you give me a mortgage? I'm not at all sure that I would give myself one.

I dig out my smartest gear and polish my battered boots in the remaining minutes before we run up the road to school. A love of polishing leather is something I have inherited from my father. It is so beautiful to see that deep molassen hue emerging as you rhythmically brush and buff.

I have an appointment with a mortgage adviser at 9am. With split second precision we descend the stone steps of our wee terraced house and run along our sleepy cobbled street, Fenning unwittingly blazing the trail in his buckled buggy (of course he can walk, but this is faster).

Rounding the corner onto Glenogle Road we suddenly enter the bustle and congestion of city life. Impatient faces peer from queues of exhaust spewing cars. It's faster on foot, I grin at them.

Once I have seen my three boys safely in to their classrooms I stride up the steep incline to the New Town area of Edinburgh and arrive on George Street flushed with exertion and with not a moment to spare.

Several hours later I emerge into the city sunshine, my brain overloaded with facts and figures. Base rates, discount rates, fixed rates, variable rates, tracker rates. They all seem to me to be extortionately high rates. I have filled in numerous forms, produced copious evidence of my identity and drunk lethal quantities of café latte.

I drift along George Street, trying hard to not even look in to those sumptuous shops oozing expensive linen, silk and cashmere. The first buds of spring cheer me as I pass Queen Street Gardens and head for home. All I can do now is wait and see if any one of those big lenders will accept me as a big spender.

At 5pm some good friends call round. They are also seeking a mortgage so we compare notes, share a bottle of wine and then decide to head out for some food with our collective brood of children.

At the last moment Miles reminds me it's Cubs night and that he is being "invested". I wish this was something which could make us some money but instead it seems to involve me giving him £3.50. We take Miles up the road then shop for food (so why are we in the off-licence?).

Later I collect a joyously over the moon Miles, proudly sporting a yellow neckerchief and clutching a fistful of badges (to be sewn on to my cub uniform, Mum).

Back at our friends' house we end the evening with a home viewing of Chitty Chitty Bang Bang (we even sing along). My boys and I walk home along cobbled streets under a clear starry sky, Fenning curling in to sleep on my back.

Next morning I have escaped the busy streets with a walk to one of my favourite city places: the Botanic Gardens. I am contemplating the space where the elegant and ancient Cedar of Lebanon lived until last winter's snow storm tragically uprooted it.

The crass music of my mobile phone jolts me out of my dwam. Once I have remembered where it is and which button to press, I finally get through to the caller. Oh joy of joys, it's one of those mortgage fellas with the stunning news that they are happy to offer me a mortgage! Whoopee. We're on our way to Orkney.

~

Flittin'
~ *July*

We're moving house and I can see why this is said to be amongst the most stressful of life's events: topped only by marriage and bereavement I believe.

The huge Orcadian removal lorry gets stuck in our narrow Edinburgh street. When all else fails I organise the gathered onlookers to lift a small car out of the way (thank goodness it doesn't have an alarm) to give the lorry the extra space it needs. With the lorry successfully out, we carefully replace the car in its original space. No harm done and owner none the wiser.

The boys request that we leave Edinburgh via the Forth Road Bridge. This is a brilliant idea. As we climb high over the Forth I have a strong sense of leaving one life behind me and heading North to a new beginning. The boys yell "Bye-bye Edinburgh" and "Briiiiiiiiiiiddge".

So we are travelling up the A9 once again, this time in a 1978 Series III Landrover. This is the first vehicle I have ever felt excited about. As with the house in Orkney, the Landy wasn't exactly for sale when I decided to try and buy it. It was parked on our walking route to school so twice a day we had the chance to admire it. After a few months we were saying "there's our Landy" and eventually Miles suggested that we put a wee note on the windscreen asking if it could be ours, please. That worked.

The back is packed from floor to ceiling with plant pots, camping gear, a hoover, Lego, clothes, wellies, four footballs, a small Rowan tree, large containers of diesel oil and water and several box loads of things I forgot to send in the removal lorry. Plus the essential family travel survival kit (containing plasters, juice, junk food, story tapes, cards, cuddly toys and ready mixed G&T).

In the rear view mirror I can see a fluffy elephant. The side view mirrors have been shaken well off course – Landrovers are not designed for smooth travel. I rejoice at the clear road with no caravans or lorries up ahead until Miles counts the number of vehicles behind us. Oops. With a top cruising speed of 40mph I guess we are holding a few people up.

Through my own lack of planning, we have a month in hand before we can move in to our new house. We want to be in Orkney to get to know folk before school starts so I think that I have booked a holiday cottage to span this time. However we have a much better welcome in store than I could have anticipated as the holiday cottage owners invite us to stay with them instead. What better introduction to the island.

The boys are whisked off to football, beach trips, parties and school summer activities so that by the time they start school they know most of their classmates. I meet lots of lovely people, take a crash course in understanding the strong Orcadian dialect (I still find myself guessing and trying to lip-read sometimes) and learn some of the low-down on island life.

Our house warming present from these wonderfully welcoming neighbours is a sack of barley, seven chickens, fifty turf sods and a wall. Just what I always wanted.

~

Illustration by Emma Grove

Ferry-Loupers
~ Autumn
2001

Goods & Chattels
~ *September*

Our furniture arrives at our new home in several loads, whenever the local haulier can bring it across on the ferry. This is brilliant because a) I'm not overwhelmed with boxes and b) it feels a bit like Christmas, wondering what might arrive next. The only drawback is that life's essentials (the corkscrew for instance) remain perversely absent until the very last delivery.

Friends from Orkney Mainland come over to help with the flitting and arrive with their motorbike laden with tools. Within 48 hours they have dismantled the kitchen units, lugged the carpets out to cover the weed-choked vegetable garden, built a loft bed for Miles (I would have scratched my head over the instructions for a month), plumbed in the washing machine and clipped many yards of fuchsia hedge. On their last afternoon they actually manage a quick whizz around the island on their bike.

The final delivery is by far the most exciting. My brother and his family arrive after two days of travel with their horse, Chuck, who is to live here with us. Despite his name I am assured that he is a very good natured and well-behaved horse. He kicks up his heels with delight and rolls in the long grass of my back field.

Now I have more visitors to put to work. Tasks completed over the following four days include fixing the hen house turf roof and installing nesting boxes and roosting bars, clearing the byres of decades of accumulated "might come in handy one day" stuff, filling pot holes in the track, de-weeding the yard to expose beautiful flagstones, fixing up a clothes pulley over the stove and painting the hall.

Meanwhile the boys make dens and secret passages through the overgrown garden. Once again it is not until their last afternoon that I allow my family some time off to look around the island. There's no rest for visitors here.

School starts. The boys know so many people by now that they are excited rather than nervous about their first day. Miles cycles down to the road and leaves his bike resting on the fence in company with five others while he hops on to the school bus.

On school days there are kids' bikes left at roadsides all over the island, providing visual testimony to the freedom of life here. Nobody would dream of having to padlock them. Similarly I have neither taken the keys out of our Landrover nor locked the house door since we arrived. Thus one significant source of stress in modern day life has been removed.

Dale, who at five years old is definitely the loudest person in our house, becomes silent and pensive in school. In the city school this change of character went unnoticed, but here everyone knows everyone else both in and out of school. By the end of the first week Dale is so surrounded by familiar faces and friends that he cannot resist joining in. His sombre expression gives way to a cheeky grin and eyes full of mirth.

I won't go into detail about what else we have encountered at our new school, but I can tell you that nit combs are excellent for getting paint out of your hair.

~

Kye
~ *September*

The sun is high in a clear blue sky. A fresh South-westerly breeze pushes at our backs as we slip-slide our way across the kelp-strewn rocks of the causeway, negotiable only at low tide. We are heading out to a tidal island to shift cows back to their home farm. This surely is a fine afternoon to be out and I am very pleased to have been asked to help.

With the cattle gathered up, two of us head back across the causeway, sixty cows following obediently behind us. Once on the road the more boisterous cows think they should be in the lead – they know where they are going better than I do – and I tell them off but wonder what I am supposed to do if they really make a break for it. Twenty years ago I had a job droving cattle in Australia. We worked using horses, motorbikes and a helicopter. Now, walking along on foot, I feel vulnerable and I can't see why these cows should obey me.

Two hours later we have successfully made our way along the coast road and herded the cattle in to their new field. Throughout the walk I have had glorious views across the sea to other islands. I have had the wind and sun in my face. I have had the sights and sounds of curlew, redshank, lapwing and oystercatcher feeding in the fields and flitting along the sand dunes. I feel steeped in the beauty and tranquility of this place. I am also hot, tired, hungry and very thirsty. We head back to the farmer's home where I am given food, beer and my children back.

I am still fairly ignorant of the wildlife here and haven't yet found time to don binoculars and look around. The closest I have come to birdlife so far was the morning I opened the front door to find a young fulmar on our doorstep. It looked quizzically at me, head tilted, then turned and walked away. I was obviously not what it had hoped for. It hung around the yard for two days and I thought it must be injured but could not catch it to get a closer look. On day three it took off, flying without trouble and looking perfectly healthy, and headed for the coast.

The school head teacher tells me that they have had ducks nesting in the middle of the playground (deftly dodging footballs until six ducklings hatched out) not to mention the one found running up the main corridor, the janitor and a parent in hot pursuit. A herd of cows once strayed in to the playground. A neighbour tells of the puffin who ran into his house seeking refuge from a cat.

I have been advised to keep the hens shut in at night, not because of foxes, which are absent from this island, but in case any of the island's otters come looking for food. We see seals every time we go to the beach and they swim towards us, curious rather than scared. Skeins of geese fly overhead and land in the fields to feed. When driving anywhere, one must allow time for the possibility of travelling in first gear behind a herd of cattle or flock of sheep for a while. The close proximity of animals – both wild and farmed – is a part of life here.

~

Autumn Homesteading
~ *October*

I'm lying full length on the kitchen floor scraping up some very old and incredibly well stuck linoleum tiles. I was on my knees until my feet went numb. Our new collie pup thinks the scraper is for catching and I am for climbing on and biting. Those playful puppy bites that leave punctures in your skin and tears in your eyes. Tom Waits croons "Somewhere" at me from the CD player. I take regular swigs from a glass (well, a Bonne Maman jam jar actually – stemmed glasses fall over too easily) of wine by my side. It's a regular Saturday night in for this single Mum.

The weather has turned wild and wet so I have abandoned my garden for the time being, in favour of some "housework". At the moment this does not involve duster and polish but ladder, hammer, screwdriver, scraper and paintbrush. The walls are in good condition so I can get straight to the fun of painting on some bright colours. Capsicum red, Wedgwood blue, emerald green and Saharan gold. Shocking taste, I know, but you need some hot colours inside when it's fridgey-cold out.

Miles wants an entirely underwater scene in his bedroom, with the water's surface up at his loft-bed level (so that he can breathe). I'm not sure that my artistic skills are quite up to bottlenose dolphins, basking sharks and giant turtles (no, we are not going to be geographically correct with our choice of species). Luckily my nieces painted on a fabulously pink giant octopus and a fearsomely toothed shark during their visit, so we're off to a good start. The bed must of course become a boat. A ferryboat or a fishing boat – we haven't decided yet.

True to form, Dale and Fenning cannot agree between pillarbox red and lime green for their shared bedroom (I made the mistake of allowing them free choice from the colour charts). At five and

four years old respectively, arguing is a favourite sport for these two brothers. Their eloquence astounds me at times as they home in on the opposite extremes of a subject with all the wit and alacrity of debating society leaders. At other times of course they rapidly resort to whacking each other over the head like true Vikings (as I suspect debating society members would do if it were allowed). To put a stop to this particular argument I am doing two walls of each colour and I'll just have to wear sunglasses whenever I go in there.

As soon as the weather clears I am back outside. There is just so much to do and I would rather be out than in. So inside we have half-painted walls and rooms without doors, but outside we have a thoroughly dug veggie plot, pruned gooseberry bushes and mown grass.

On Sunday morning I shift a tonne of coal, from the yard where it was delivered, into the byre next to the house. The boys help for about three minutes then decide a game of hide and seek with the puppy would be much more fun. Thanks guys. On a Sunday morning in Edinburgh I would have been munching croissant, sipping café latte and delving into the papers while the boys watched a video. Some changes then.

~

Tonight there is a proper night out in store for us. Once a year the Screen Machine visits our island. This fantastic beast is a lorry with a cinema on its back. With 102 seats and five screenings of three different films on offer over its two day visit, there is the opportunity for everyone on the island to enjoy a trip to the flicks. This time our choices are "Shrek", "The Parole Officer" and "Bridget Jones' Diary". How long ago were these films showing in the city?

It's tipping down with rain as folk arrive at the lay-by where the Screen Machine has chosen to park. Popcorn, juice, crisps and ice-lollies are sold from the back of someone's car to raise money for the school PTA. The ticket office is in the lorry's cab.

The atmosphere inside the cinema is jolly (not to mention damp) as neighbours greet each other and peel off dripping jackets. My children seek out their friends to sit beside, not needing to be with me for security.

Five minutes in to the film the mechanism breaks down. Ah well, a chance for more chat and it's handy to have the lights up again while we work on these rather tightly knotted bags of popcorn. Once the driver/ticket seller/film mechanic has fixed the problem everyone settles down again for the rest of the film.

This is a highly sophisticated travelling cinema. I once encountered a very different set up at a small fishing village on the island of Zanzibar (off the coast of Tanzania, East Africa). It consisted of a TV set propped on the tailgate of a Landrover and wired up to its battery. The auditorium was the village's football pitch – an area of sun-scorched grassland and red earth.

The audience (of several hundred) sat on the ground munching sunflower seeds and spitting out the seed cases. Those at the front gave a running commentary on the plot and the information was passed through the audience to the back. Even if you could see the TV, there was no way of hearing it because the Landrover engine had to be kept running. After a while someone took the TV off the tailgate, where it was vibrating in time with the engine, and put it on the ground.

As the hot sun dipped below the horizon a gentle onshore breeze cooled us. We jeered the bad guys and cheered the good guys (it was a "Rambo" film so this was easy) and everyone had a fine time. The money raised from Coke and sunflower seeds was given to the local school to buy jotters and pencils.

Despite the different levels of sophistication (and the contrast in weather conditions!) our trip to the Screen Machine reminds me of that evening in Africa. It is good fun watching a film surrounded by people you know. Popcorn tastes much better when you know that you are helping to raise funds for your school (but next time can it be salty please?). While living on far-flung islands the wars of the world seem mercifully remote.

~

Boys across Scotland
~ *October*

I am forlorn. School is out and the boys have gone to see their father in the Hebrides for two weeks. You might think that I would welcome a break from the arduous task of bringing up three boys. I did think that myself. But the reality is that my life revolves around the children.

My days are filled with their need to be nurtured, organised, taxied around, entertained and, above all, loved. They are also my company and my best friends. So when they are not with me I feel unbalanced, out of kilter and very alone.

For the boys this is a big trip. Their journey takes them on three ferryboats and across 300 miles of north and west Scotland. I travel with them to Orkney Mainland then a good friend takes them on to Inverness where they meet up with Dad.

This leaves me with a day in Kirkwall, one of the two main towns in Orkney. I wander along the narrow, flagstone streets, home in on a bookshop for a while, visit St Magnus Cathedral (an astonishingly beautiful building), get my hair cut and have lunch with a friend. It's all very pleasant and a good change of scene but I am really happy when the time comes to get on the boat which will take me back home.

There is plenty to do with my boy-free time. I want to finish painting their bedrooms, unblock the drain in the yard, and find a hen that my friend's dog chased away down the field. I plan to get out riding on Chuck more and explore different parts of the island. I might even make it to the pub one evening.

Meanwhile my neighbouring farmer brings four tractor loads of straw over and together we unload and stack 80 bales in to the end byre. The builder delivers half of the floorboarding needed to cover the ground floor of the house and we stack that in the near byre.

Also there is the chance to relax a bit, perhaps even have a lie-in. I try this on my first morning alone. At 7am the puppy whines to be let out. I sleepwalk my way down the stairs thinking: dog out, make cup of tea, back to bed.

Storm and Omelette (our cats – named by Dale and Fenning respectively) yeowl at me on the doorstep. So I feed them, which involves going out to the byre. From here I can see Chuck leaning over the gate speaking volumes with his pricked ears and yearning eyes. Oh all right then: I measure out some horse feed then trudge out to the field to give it to Chuck and take off his night rug.

By this time I am frozen to the bone (I'm only in my raggedy old pyjamas, my bare feet pushed in to wellies) but think I may as well keep going and let the hens out. I finally make it back to bed with a cup of tea. Five minutes later the phone rings and I have to run back downstairs. It's my Mum to see if I'm OK – she knows how sad I get when the boys are away. I decide to take a long hot bath.

~

Deserted Sandy Beaches

~ October

A deserted sandy beach is my all time favourite place to be. It is an environment where I can clear my head, breathe easy and think fresh thoughts. I don't care what the weather is like although given a choice I would prefer wild and windy to still and hot. With these preferences, Orkney is a great place to be.

My children love beaches too, but we have rather different agendas. Theirs is to find a good digging spot as fast as possible and then stay there and dig...for hours. I like to walk the length of the beach, combing for treasures and staring with tireless fascination at the sea.

These would not be mutually exclusive activities if I could be sure that the boys would stay on the beach. But they cannot resist the lure of the sea. Seemingly undaunted by any weather conditions, Fenning is always the first to dispense with his clothing and leap naked into the freezing waves. Miles and Dale do that most annoying of things: run in to the water fully clad then run back up the beach to peel off their wet clothes and dump them in a sandy heap.

The last time they indulged in a skinny-dip was earlier this month. I laughed at their sheer madness (safe in my cocoon of warm clothing) and ushered them back to the Landy, where I now keep a permanent supply of towels and spare clothes.

This week the boys are still away with their father so I can enjoy some beach trips without the worry of hypothermic children. I make several trips to our nearest beach on Chuck. To begin with he was extremely suspicious of the sea. What was this beast which roared and rushed toward him? My niece was riding him and I watched as they pranced their way along the sands, dancing to the rhythm of the waves. Chuck's hooves left the pattern of a heartbeat along the waterline as he leapt further up the beach with every approaching wave then moved cautiously back down again with the water's retreat. Now he is happy to visit the beach and only occasionally snorts at a pile of seaweed, an old fishbox or an abandoned boot. We follow the strand line, cantering into the wind and both loving the freedom.

Today the island is enveloped in a low mist so I decide to leave Chuck in his field – he would spook at every fencepost in this weather – and take Swan (our collie pup) to a different stretch of coast. We leave the Landrover where the road peters out and wind our way through a narrow strip of sand dunes. Swan is distracted by a myriad of rabbit burrows. I reach the edge of the dunes and can just make out a fabulous sweep of pale sand through the mist.

Two ravens fly up from a rabbit carcass at the sight of me. Cackling gulls wheel overhead. Swan and I go down to the water's edge and she leaps back and forth, allowing the waves to chase her. Walking east we can suddenly make out the dark forms of about 50 seals hauled up on the sand. They stay put until we are within 20 metres then lunge and plunge into the sea. This beach may be devoid of other humans, but deserted it is not. I feel I am intruding on the privacy of its inhabitants.

~

Weet
~ October

The boys are home. This is their first day back at school for the winter term. I get them up at 6am by mistake (having forgotten all about the BST to GMT change). It has been raining all weekend and the yard is several inches deep in water. I try to start the Landrover and it responds with a pathetic cough, a dull whirr, then silence. Dismal.

The upside, now that it is officially winter, is that the school bus comes to the bottom of our track instead of just to the nearest main road. So we all run through squalls of rain leaping around the muddy puddles and reach the bus, which is by now reversing up our track. "Would you like a lift to nursery with Fenning?" are the bus driver's words as I open the side door. So in those few minutes of watching us run down the track she has worked out what is wrong and how she can help. Her thoughtfulness lifts my flagging spirits.

Fenning is delighted: he has never been on the school bus before. He counts the seats, counts the windows, counts the other children and attempts to count the time left until he'll be in Primary One and on this bus every day. The concept of ten months is hard for a four-year-old so I try telling him that it will be after next summer. In this weather the concept of "summer" is quite hard for both of us. He is not quite so pleased with the speed with which I deposit him at his nursery and leap back on the bus for a ride home (luckily the driver is also a near neighbour).

By amazing good fortune my AA membership is still in date (it has usually just lapsed when my vehicles break down). At 10am the AA tells me that their Kirkwall representative will be with me by 10.40am. "Kirkwall is an hour and a half away by boat and the next boat is not until this evening", I feel compelled to mention. But the telephonist merely repeats that their mechanic will be with me in 40 minutes. I am intrigued. Perhaps the AA has a speedboat service for awkward places like this, or has sussed time travel.

While I am waiting for the AA spacecraft (or whatever) to arrive I decide to tackle the blocked drain in the yard. I suspect that the drain is under an old Belfast sink that is propped on bricks under the yard tap. The sink proves to be astonishingly heavy, the submerged flagstones which I am standing on prove to be very slippery and my left welly proves to have sprung a leak.

The rain descends with renewed vigour. I seek refuge in the house, only to discover that the porch roof is leaking. At some point this *will* become a good day.

At 10.30am one of the island mechanics arrives having had a phone call from the Kirkwall AA garage. Mystery solved and no UFO's involved. The Landrover's problem turns out to be a flat battery and the culprit a hopelessly loose fan belt. So that's what has been whining at me for the last few weeks. Well – I never was any good at car maintenance.

~

Harvest Hame
~ November

Through all this nasty wintry weather I have been communing with my garden rather more than I would like. Our bathroom needed to be re-fitted and I asked the builders to do it while my sons were away with their father.

To their credit they achieved exactly that (and how often can you say that about builders). On Sunday afternoon they ripped out the old bathroom suite. On Monday they scratched their heads over the rather weird plumbing routes through the house. Over the following two days my new bath, sink and loo were installed.

These of course are not new at all (don't be silly) but are even older than those they are replacing. I am now the proud owner of a rusting enamelled metal tub, a chunky ceramic sink whose hot tap drips and a grass-stained loo. In their defence, they came "free to a good home" out of someone's garden. And aesthetically they please me like mustard yellow plastic just never could.

The work was "finished" (this is builder-speak for a job that is 90% complete and mostly functional: when the finishing touches will be achieved is anybody's guess) the evening before I collected Miles, Dale and Fenning. At 10pm all I had to do was apply three coats of varnish to the new floor-boards. I managed the first coat by midnight (there was a lot of dust to hoover up first), the second coat at 5am and the final coat at 10am before zooming down to the pier to catch the ferry. I could have stomached the rough crossing if I hadn't been suffering a varnish sniffer's hangover.

According to the instructions on the tin the newly varnished floor was not to be subjected to "heavy traffic" for 24 hours. In my estimation three small boys and their incumbent plastic dinosaurs etc. qualify as heavy traffic so I denied them access to the loo for a day. This was easy because a) they like peeing in the garden anyway and b) when we got back to the island that evening we went straight to a dance.

The dinner-dance was the annual "Harvest Hame" – a self-explanatory title. Ticketed to start at 8pm, the boys and I arrived fashionably late at twenty past to find everybody already seated and tucking in to the main course. A hush fell as we wended our way between the tables searching in vain for four places together. Eventually we were squeezed in but it is obviously not the done thing to arrive late. I'll know next time.

For dinner we were introduced to the delights of clapshot: a mash of tattie and turnip enhanced with butter and onions. This traditional Orkney dish was followed by speeches. The boys weathered these with amazing patience given that not all of them achieved what the first speaker suggested was the measure of a good speech ("akin to a dress: long enough to cover the subject, short enough to be interesting" ho ho). Finally, after much clearing and shifting of tables, the dance began.

Orkney dances are wilder versions of Scottish Country dances. Rather than taking it in turns everyone whirls around at once. As the majority of folk here have been dancing since birth, they know the steps and can keep the rhythm however much hooch has been imbibed. I won't tell you what time I got the boys to bed but I will admit that they were still happily dancing at midnight.

~

Chambered Cairn
~ *November*

There's a saying about Orkney that you only have to scratch the surface to find signs of previous lives. It is an archaeologist's mecca. This morning I decide to take a walk to a chambered cairn (a communal tomb dating back to 3000 BC) set on a peninsula to the south of the island.

Once the boys are at school I drive south then turn onto a pot-holed track. Most journeys on this island involve a pot-holed track at some point. My immediate view is of a small sea inlet – the "Peedie Sea" as it is called here – sheltered by long limbs of land. The track runs parallel to the shoreline where oystercatcher, redshank and dunlin search and probe for food. Wigeon duck and dive out in the bay.

A right fork in the track leads to the shore. At low tide one can drive across the sands, but this morning the tide is high and the route off limits so I stick to the high road. With the track still hugging the edge of the Peedie Sea on my right, the land to my left drops away to reveal a sweep of sand edging the ice-blue ocean. The track ends at the further end of this isthmus and it is time to park and walk.

I can see my destination immediately. The cairn has been prominently placed on the eastern edge of this long spit of land. The dogs (we now have a second puppy – a collie/spaniel mixture that I couldn't resist and which the boys have bizarrely named HotDog) and I set off along the coastal path.

A freezing northerly wind urges us on and I am already aware of the struggle we will have walking back. As we head south of the sandy bay I remember bringing the boys here last summer. We had set off to visit the cairn then, but the heat of the day and the lure of the beach overcame us and we headed down for a swim instead. Today that decision is hard to comprehend.

Turnstone flit among the rocks and seaweed. The path deteriorates into a cattle-poached quagmire. Sleet pounds at my back. As the tomb looms ahead a feeling of disorientation engulfs me. I find it hard to contemplate a time span of 5000 years since this structure was built.

The dogs have no intention of entering the low (less than three foot), dark passage and whine desperately at me as I crawl along its thirty foot length to the inner chamber. I squat on the earth floor and peer in to the six side chambers.

Bones of at least 10 adults and five children were found in this tomb, along with animal bones, bone and stone tools and pottery fragments. I feel calm and at ease in here, not spooked as I thought I might. A sense of peace hangs in the still, quiet air. I think this would be a rather beautiful place to be laid to rest.

As I emerge from the tunnel a shrill noise sends my heart leaping. It's my mobile phone bringing me back to the 21st century with an ugly jolt. We head for home, the wind driving hail mercilessly into our faces. I tuck HotDog inside my jacket – she's a tired wee pup.

~

Bathtub Enamelling
~ *November*

This has got to stop. I really must refrain from sniffing mind-altering chemical substances. My poison this time is enamel paint and there seem to be no "low odour" varieties of this noxious liquid. So this is my penance for choosing to introduce an old and rusty bathtub into my life.

My first task was to track down a source for a bath enamel kit. I was drawing a blank with the friends and family "word of mouth" search system. Then someone suggested searching via the internet. This took me by surprise because, despite being all linked up (and that concept blows my mind right from the start – I still don't understand the telephone system), I never ever think of using the internet for anything. I'm sure I have been born into the wrong century.

Once my nine year old son had helped me to link up to the net (see, I don't even know the jargon) I typed in "bath enamel" with a large degree of scepticism. But, after some chuntering, two listings appeared with offers to sell me a "Tubby DIY Kit" there and then, on screen. I couldn't quite bring myself to do that so I jotted down their telephone numbers, wound down the computer and phoned them up. Where's the logic in that?

I felt a great sense of achievement when the kit arrived in the post a few days later. Somehow that seemed to be enough achievement for the time being and I didn't actually open the box for several weeks. Then, having never enamelled a bathtub, I thought I had better read the instructions (usually a last resort). These proved so daunting that the whole kit was parked on a shelf again and has been glaring at me ever since. Now, finally, I must get the job done.

First I get all of us to take a bath because the tub will be out of action for two days once I have painted it. Then, boys pyjama'd and tucked up in bed, I scrub the bath with the provided cleaning powder. After that I scrub it again – it is shamefully grubby.

Point two in the instructions demands that I sand the surface with abrasive paper (two sheets provided) until it has "worn through completely". This requires so much elbow grease (none provided) that I wonder about the wording of the instructions. Who is supposed to be worn through completely? The old enamel, the sandpaper or me?

Two sheets of sandpaper later the tub is snow white and no longer looks as if it needs re-enamelling. However I'm certainly not giving up now. The paint needs to be applied in a warm, well-ventilated, dust-free room. Orkney weather makes this quite hard to achieve. Opening a window introduces a small gale into the room that reduces the air temperature by several degrees per second and liberates dust from every nook and cranny. I settle for warm and dust free – two out of three ain't bad – and resign myself to inhaling the fumes.

Three hours and two paint coats later I stretch my aching back and proudly survey my dazzling bathtub. The gleaming surface looks good as new. Meanwhile I am sweaty and exhausted. What I could really do with now is a bath.

~

Filling our days
~ *November*

A friend from London recently asked me how I fill my days on this island: a place where she cannot imagine what there is to do. Once I had stopped laughing I gave her a run down of our average week.

I wake to the sound of Dale going downstairs for a pee and to let the dogs out. Then he comes in to my bed for a cuddle and to mention that he is hungry. Miles clambers from his loft bed like a sloth from a tree.

While the boys are finding socks and eating breakfast I am out feeding the horse, cats and hens and mucking out the stable. At regular intervals I head back to the kitchen to check progress and offer helpful advice ("eat your banana!" "tie your laces!" "hurry up!!" and so on). With much prompting Miles achieves clothes, food, brushed teeth, school bag and jacket. He heads off down the track in time for the 8.30am bus.

Dale dresses quickly and concentrates on eating everything in sight. He is the hungriest person I know (except, perhaps, me) and I am already wondering how I will cater for him through his teenage years. The vegetable plot grows ever larger in my mind's eye.

Fenning is a sleepy head and more often than not I have to dress him while he lies in bed, carry him out to the Landrover and put a flapjack in his hand. The second bus run picks Dale up at 9.20am after which I drive Fenning to nursery.

While the boys are at school I whiz around digging the garden, painting walls, hanging washing or whatever. My latest project is to varnish the pile of floorboards out in the byre, before they are laid in the kitchen. Chuck and I ride to the beach for an hour or so with the dogs, and often the cats, running along behind. Then there's some writing to fit in. I also try to find time to clear out my workshop and set it up as a pottery. Working with clay is what I actually aim to do when I find some time. I'll let you know...

The school bus deposits my boys home at 3.10pm. That's assuming no after school activities. These are plentiful and tax my memory to its limit. On Monday Miles has cookery and must be collected at 4.15pm. On Tuesday Dale swims 2.45pm until 3.45pm. Wednesday is Football Club between 6pm and 7.30pm. Fiddle Club is on Thursday immediately after school. Miles and Dale also have fiddle lessons during school time and at some point each week I have a lesson too (it's one of those "things to do before you are 40", don't you think?).

Friday is a double whammy – swimming for Fenning and First Aid for Miles. On Saturday afternoon we all go swimming. Youth Club is on Saturday evening so we go to the pub for a chip supper and a game of pool first. Sunday is beach day – I need a blast of salt air on my face.

There are even more activities that the boys could take part in, but their taxi driver is exhausted. I am by no means the busiest person here, or anywhere else in the world for that matter, but my days are full enough, thank you.

~

Batten Down
The Hatches

~ Winter
2001/2002

Kelp
~ December

The driving force of the ocean can change the character of a stretch of coastline overnight. I am in awe of the sheer energy and power with which the sea can shift sand dunes or carve caves into rocks or fling a wrecked ship or a whale carcass onto a sweep of sand.

The islanders have always made good use of the flotsam and jetsam of the ocean. It is said that the people here used to pray for shipwrecks, which provided wood for building or burning plus the unknown bonus of whatever cargo was on board (and maybe even some sailors to marry and turn into farmers!). In my byre are about 50 neatly stacked wooden pit props – the remnants of a massive load shed by a cargo ship passing the island a few years ago. Not as exciting as "Whiskey Galore" but probably more useful.

Every time we return to our local beach it has altered. Sometimes the changes are subtle – a shift in the lie of the sand or a deposit of larger shells and pebbles. The storms of a few weeks ago brought a dramatic change. The next time we made our way along the Ware Road – the name of the coastal track that leads us to this beach - we halted at the edge of the dunes, shocked by the black shore. A "ware brack" – a whole heap of seaweed ("tangles") – had been washed ashore and piled high along the length of the bay.

For Orkney, seaweed has been a big money spinner in the past. It is a rich source of potash, soda, iodine and alginates. Kelp (the product of burning seaweed) export was big business in the 18th and 19th centuries to cater for the needs of soap and glass industries and tangles were exported for alginate extraction until the end of the 20th century.

I have recently been lent a great wee book called "Kelp-making in Orkney" by William Thomson so on the occasions when I get the boys to bed and still have some energy (not often) I read a bit. In the last week I have learnt that those seaweeds growing between high and low water mark, are known as "tang" whereas those growing at or below low tide are known as "ware". Tang and ware come in many forms – bow-tang, paddy-tang, prickly tang, mirkle, honey-ware, hen-ware. Tang is rich in potash and soda. The "tangle" (long stalk) of ware is laden with iodine. Where is my biology degree now?

Imagine you are a kelp-maker. To make kelp first drag your tang or ware up the beach. Lay the strands out to dry then burn them in pit kilns for many hours. Whenever a gale brings a ware brack ashore, be it autumn, winter or spring, then everyone, including children, must work to drag the tangles inland to dry for kelp or to fertilise your farmland.

But the best time to gather tang is in the summer, between the spring crop sowing and autumn haymaking. To make use of the long hours of daylight you must work from 2am to 11pm, occasionally stopping to eat, take a nap or dry your feet. It is cold, wet toil and much less fun than your predecessor's annual summer activity of launching Viking raids on neighbouring islands. And to add insult to injury, your laird pockets the considerable profits.

~

Miles' Birthday
~ December

Miles is ten today. His ten year old desires include the Beano Manual 2002, a gold hoop in his left ear, a razor short hair cut, a "Stomp Rocket", any Harry Potter merchandise, a proper grown-up wrist watch and a pair of "Ridiculous Flashing Glasses" with battery operated windscreen wipers. He has reached that age when the lure of the adult world contends with a continued desire for childish toys (and do we ever really grow out of it?).

His other wish is for a swimming party and this wish is being granted this afternoon. I spend all morning baking chocolate frogs and grilling sausages. Armed with box loads of food and drink (wine included, of course) we set off down the road to our island swimming pool.

The existence of a pool here gives testimony to the strong community spirit. It was opened in 1993, the culmination of less than three years of fund raising by a population of less than 600 people. Money came in from all over the world, residents dug deep into their own pockets and some pretty original fund raising events were enacted. Islanders, many of whom could not swim - on an island surrounded by icy seas this is hardly surprising – subsequently learnt and can now enjoy a sport whatever the weather. Children are encouraged to learn from an early age, with lots of extra sessions for school kids.

As well as the school swimming programme and any private sessions, there are eight scheduled pool sessions per week. Each one requires the attendance of two lifeguards and a "keyholder" (someone to open up the Community Building, supervise proceedings and sell the inevitable crisps and sweeties). A group of committed volunteers fill these posts as well as attending ongoing lifeguarding and first aid training sessions.

Miles is sharing his party with a girl in his class whose birthday falls on the same day. This arrangement has the great advantage that an even mix of boys and girls has been invited, without the embarrassment of a boy inviting a girl, or vice versa. The fifteen guests range in age from fourteen to four. With a school role of less than 80 – and that includes nursery, primary and secondary classes – all the children know each other. Indeed, as Primary Six consists of six girls plus Miles, his male friends are all in different years.

Once in the pool the kids organise themselves into teams and play a series of frenetic ball games with much splashing, shouting, plunging on top of each other and general hilarity. They are not keen for us "Mums" to interfere with their fun so we retreat to the deep end, swim widths and chat. Our lifeguards today are a teacher and a nurse respectively - both well practised at exerting authority. The kids know they won't get away with any bad behaviour.

Afterwards there is just time to consume the mass of party food which we have assembled in the Community Hall, sing, blow out candles and demolish the Hogwart's Castle cake (what else could it be, this year?) before it is time for everyone to go home. All in all a pretty stress free party and our house wasn't trashed in the process.

~

Christmas
~ *December*

How did Christmas creep up on me like that? I feel as if I have only just moved in and yet here we are in the throes of Christmas parties, school concerts and a plethora of Orkney style knees-ups.

When we moved, at the height of last summer, I envisaged being super organised for our first Christmas here – freshly decorated, book-lined rooms, re-covered sofas, tasteful lighting, curtains, floorboards. That sort of thing. Then I imagined all the baking and other fancy food preparation I would achieve, whilst also relaxing for some quality time with my children over the holidays. Delusions of Domestic Goddess status, perhaps?

Well, we are sort of half way there with all of these things. Our rooms are half-painted – ceilings and skirtings are such a bore. Curtains never seem to get to the top of the priority list and with nearest neighbours half a mile away we hardly need them for privacy. The floorboards are still stacked in the byre (so we have, at least, got them). It could be said that we have book-lined rooms but a more accurate description would portray boxes of books concealed behind sofas and under side-lamps. Shelving is one of those things I haven't quite got my head around just yet.

With two puppies assiduously chewing the furniture (despite repeated applications of Tabasco sauce to all the corners) there seems little point in new coverings for awhile yet. Indeed I suspect re-upholstery may be required by the time they are grown dogs. The only electrician here has a waiting list longer than the length of the island, so my new lighting desires will have to wait.

In the baking department, after the first month four-year-old Fenning gave up asking me when a cake would appear out of our exciting new food mixer. In the last week it has been dusted off and pressed into action (definitely no time to read the instructions and find out what all the extra attachments do) to create batches of buns and cookies. Fenning has watched in dismay as these get bundled into tins and whisked out of sight. These, of course, are for the many Christmas functions to which everyone brings something savoury and something sweet. My "savoury" is pizza and my "sweet" is chocolate brownies. This is the full extent of my culinary repertoire. At any rate I would not want any of my other kitchen creations to be exposed to public scrutiny.

I am proud to announce that I *have* been super-organised in the present department. Having lived on islands before, I have present buying down to a fine art. I order everything through mail order catalogues in October. That includes cards, wrapping paper, Christmas decorations, tins of fancy biscuits (oops, shouldn't a Goddess be making those?) and even edible Christmas stockings for the dogs and a fleecy numnah for the horse.

On this treeless island I had notions of artistically decorating lengths of driftwood. But even Christmas trees can be ordered through the local store. After eleven years with a partner who didn't "do" Christmas I am now delighted to be able to decorate my house to my heart's content. And, as I think any visitors will agree, it is certainly copiously and joyously decorated. Who cares about tasteful?

~

Death
~ *December*

The sun is shining heroically through ice-blue sky, clouds rampaging across the vast dome of our existence. Hail stones lie in the bare earth furrows of our garden. Curlew probe the soil of our fields and call longingly into the freezing wind. The red cliffs of our neighbouring island rise out of a restless sea.

From my kitchen window I look north to the surging coils of surf crashing and rolling over The Riv – a long spit of skerries which form the most northerly point of this island. At regular intervals the cloud swirls low over the house and we are pelted with hail and horizontally driven sleet. It is Christmas Eve and God but this is a wild and beautiful place to be.

And yet I am crying. A few nights ago a friend and fellow islander died, inexplicably, in her sleep. She was my age (we joked, only last weekend, about being respectively the right and wrong side of 40) with sons aged five and eight. I was, and remain, shocked to the core at this tragedy. Where is the sense in it?

Once again the compassion and resourcefulness of this small community amazed me. Her boys were immediately taken to a friend's home and stayed there while their father made his horrendous journey from his ship off the coast of Nigeria all the way home to Orkney. The decision was made to go ahead with the Community Christmas Tree party for the children – they all needed the reassurance of some semblance of normality. But the dance the next evening was cancelled – we were hardly in the mood for a knees-up. The morning plane scheduled to fly to the island to our north diverted its journey especially to drop off a friend of her husband to the airfield here. My heart goes out to her family at this awful time.

My only comfort is that my abiding image of this good person is of her laughing and singing and thoroughly enjoying an excellent school Christmas concert two evenings before her death. And I do mean excellent. The performance arts form a central theme of life here and huge effort goes in to teaching children music, dance and singing. In Edinburgh I found it impossible to organise music lessons for my children without incurring an overdraft. Here they were offered free music lessons (instruments provided) as soon as we arrived and are already part of the Fiddle Club (albeit scratching away at the back).

The older children, with a good few years of tuition under their belts, are astonishingly accomplished whether singing, acting or playing an instrument. The Fiddle Club Concert (another great evening out) was a highly polished performance of everything from Bach to The Beetles. I noticed an intriguing lack of self-consciousness among the children - even the teenagers - who all seemed delighted to leap on stage and do their damnedest at full volume.

Now it is 1am on Christmas morning and, despite my heavy heart, time for me to perform my Father (or should that be Mother) Christmas duties. As Dale's fourth tooth has just fallen out I will have to be a fairy too. The multi-faceted demands on our lives continue regardless of tragedy.

~

Harry Potter in Kirkwall

~ *December*

Pre-dawn and our snow-bound island is buzzing with activity. Tractors are out blazing the trail through drifts of snow along tracks and side roads. Our one snowplough concentrates on clearing the main routes.

By 8am landrovers, jeeps, lorries and intrepid cars emerge from homesteads all over the island and head off to pick up friends. Then, all vehicles full to the brim, they converge on the main road and drive in convoy toward the pier.

For us this is one of the highlights of the Christmas holidays. For today we are on a trip to Kirkwall to see "Harry Potter and the Philosopher's Stone". As the film reached Orkney in the latter part of December, this is the first opportunity for many of us to see it.

Most days only a handful of passengers board the ferry. Today there are over 100, including a large proportion of children. The ferry's small lounge is packed and takes on the atmosphere of a school party. Flasks of coffee, bottles of juice, packs of sandwiches, packets of crisps and biscuits emerge from bags. Children congregate wherever there seems to be some food action, not worried about whose parent is providing it.

The ferry calls in at one other island on our way, then docks at Kirkwall after a two-hour trip. This gives us half an hour to walk through the town centre, popping in and out of shops, and on along the slush-slippery streets to the cinema. This matinee showing has been timed especially to allow us to get home again within the day.

Once the flurry of finding row numbers, deciding who will sit next to whom and stowing jackets and bags under seats has subsided, I have a look around. The cinema is at least three-quarters full of folk from our island. It reminds me of the time when the Screen Machine (cinema on a lorry) visited us.

The film is two and a half hours long and I have four small boys (my three plus one friend) to my right. I envisage several loo trips and quite a lot of endeavouring to keep the younger boys still and quiet. However every time I look along the row I see four entranced faces staring at the screen. Even Fenning, who usually has ants in his pants, confines himself to playing with the tip-up seat once or twice. This is indeed a magic film.

Our collective verdict is a definite thumbs up. Robbie Coltrane is giant strides ahead as the favourite character. The Great Hall, Diagon Alley and the Quidditch Pitch are the most exciting locations. We agree that watching the film has not destroyed our mental images conjured from reading the books, but has actually rather enhanced them.

After some more shopping we all pile back on to the boat for the journey home. We have really drawn the short straw this time as the route takes us to two other islands before we reach our own. So for nearly three hours we have to survive the traumas of an over-heated, over-full lounge full of over-excited, over-tired children. Pure hell. There's nothing for it, once we reach home, but to head straight for the pub to recover over a pint or two and some games of pool.

~

Bonfire Night
~ *January*

Today is the 5th of January and for us this is bonfire night. Well yes, you could say we are a bit behind the times up here. But it's hard to fit everything in around both the weather and the community social calendar.

Bad weather – as in howling gales – caused the postponement of bonfire night throughout November. When December arrived and we still hadn't managed to find an evening when a) the weather was behaving itself and b) all the school children were on the island (those over 16 have to take the boat to Kirkwall for their schooling from Sunday to Friday) the decision was made to save the fireworks for Christmas.

Christmas here was accompanied by sleet, ice and snow. Just the right atmosphere for our Christmas celebrations but not so good for sending Guy up in flames. Not until tonight have the roads been ice-free and the social calendar empty. So, having enjoyed a two-month stay of execution, luck has finally run out for this traitor in our midst.

Tonight the weather is behaving itself beautifully. The wind has dropped to a conspiratorial whisper. The night sky is dark and mysterious. Our massive pyre has been built on the shores of a wide sandy inlet. Word only went out this morning that the firework display would be held tonight, but word here gets around like wildfire. Anyone still not in the know will surely notice this beacon from almost anywhere on the island.

Sure enough, more and more vehicles arrive and park along the roadside. Within half an hour there are at least 150 folk, bundled into woollies and wellies, gathered around the blaze. Pretty soon our cheeks are glowing and jackets are being peeled off as the bonfire warms us. When we tire of its leaping flames, we have the option of going for a paddle in the shallows of the sea inlet.

Biscuits, sweeties and sparklers are handed around along with apologies for the lack of hot soup. The vast quantities of this prepared for November 5th have long since been consumed.

The fireworks are set up further around the bay with a few creeks between us and them acting as a deterrent to curious children. Rockets whiz and bang to emblazon the sky and Catherine Wheels whirl and effervesce at the water's edge. But the most impressive element of this display is auditory. As each firework explodes, the bang is repeated and amplified many-fold as it echoes off the ocean all around us. Gun battles at sea spring to my mind and I can imagine the terror of invasion. It is a bizarre experience and one that the locals around me say they have not heard before either – it is usually too windy to hear anything.

Tonight's gathering heralds the end of our winter festivities. Tomorrow we must take down our Christmas decorations and prepare for school on Monday. Next week I have an appointment with 10 litres of heavy-duty floor varnish – yes my kitchen floorboards have finally been laid.

But today hasn't just been about bonfires. It is my father's 86th birthday too. Happy birthday Dad.

~

Sheep Quota
~ *January*

After two weeks of ignoring any post that does not look like a Christmas card or present my "in-tray" (the hall windowsill) is overflowing. Now I have the tedious task of sorting through it. I can tell at a glance that at least 50% of the pile will be filed in the log basket. Unfortunately junk mail finds its way to remote islands or capital cities with equal ease.

I assume that the remaining buff envelopes contain bills – and most of them do – but my eye is caught by something more interesting. This is a letter from SEERAD (Scottish Executive Environment and Rural Affairs Department) to inform me that the Sheep Quota belonging to the previous owners of my property has now been transferred to me. I am the proud new owner of SAP (Sheep Annual Premium Scheme) Quota for ten sheep.

I'll admit straight away that I know absolutely nothing about sheep except that they taste good with mint sauce. Despite having listened to Radio Four's "The Archers" for at least 20 years, I don't seem to know very much about farming at all. Another steep learning curve looms ahead.

My choices seem to be either to sell the quota to someone else, or to get ten sheep myself. If I do nothing then the government will absorb the quota back in to the national pool. As I have 24 acres of grassland that need to be managed in some respect, some grazing animals seem like a good idea.

I phone my friend and unofficial agricultural adviser who suggests that I get gimmers (18 month old sheep in lamb for the first time) or in-lamb ewes (older sheep who have already had at least one lamb) but not ewe-hogs (grown lambs who have not yet had their first pregnancy). This will mean that I don't need a tup (ram) this year (if at all – perhaps one of these can be begged, borrowed or invited over the fence when required?).

Then there is the question of breed. I head over to my farming friends for more advice. Well, I could go for a pure bred flock or for cross breeds. Suffolk, Shetland, Cheviot or Texel cross breeds: they all have pros and cons. Lighter, heavier, docile, stroppy, produce fat lambs or lots of lambs. My head spins.

Our local SEERAD office has thoughtfully sent me some bumf to get me started. The "Hill and Upland News", "Golden Rules for a Healthy Flock" and "Identification of Sheep and Goats: advice to keepers" look fairly digestible. "The Rural Stewardship Scheme" looks hefty but interesting as do the "Crofting Counties Agricultural Grants Scheme (CCAGS)" Guidance Notes. As for "The Integrated Administration and Control System (IACS) Explanatory Booklet", I think calling it a booklet is extremely optimistic – it is heavy in every sense.

Another envelope contains my "Claim for Sheep Annual Premium (SAP) 2002" form plus some handy "Notes for Guidance". Claims must be in by 4th February. Yikes. I may have to shelve my novel for a while and burn the midnight oil in company with this stack of agricultural information.

I go to bed with my head full of acronyms: SEERAD, SAP, CCAGS, IACS. Attempting to read the IACS booklet is the equivalent of counting sheep. I'm asleep within minutes.

~

Destructive Puppies
~ *January*

After a week of sanding and varnishing floorboards it has been brought to my attention that I have not been getting the puppies out enough. Their mode of communicating this has been fairly destructive. Trainers, wellies, hats and gloves have been chewed, footballs punctured and dog bedding ripped apart. They have rather helpfully thought to tear up the linoleum from the porch floor – I was about to do that anyway.

Having admonished them for their acts of destruction, we head out for a walk. Because they are absolutely the best places to be (have I mentioned that before?) we make straight for a beach. Just to the east of the island's central village is Cata Sands, a vast expanse of tidal sand flanked by a massive dune system. At low tide one can walk straight across the sand flats for more than a mile. The limb of machair (herb rich coastal sandy grassland) and high dunes that delimits the flats to their east, gradually narrows until it is a mere fifty paces wide. On the eastern side of this limb is the most glorious beach imaginable, which must stretch for a good three miles, north to south.

Fulmars take off, stiff-winged, from their grass ledges and pilot down like bomber planes to check us out. They are claiming territories for their breeding season already. Swan, the older collie pup, chases one low flier at full pelt until she is stopped in her tracks by the shock of seawater up to her neck. The fulmar lifts up and away with a cackle: a practical joke executed to perfection.

The puppies run five miles for every one of mine. As we cross the dunes a snipe lifts up from the ground and zigzags away from us. Red-breasted merganser work the coastal waters in small groups. At the far end of the beach a rocky outcrop attracts a flock of turnstone and I spot a few purple sandpiper among them. Dunlin squat on the sand in their pale grey winter plumage.

At the far end of the dunes stands a big old house resplendent with archways, courtyards and a magnificent horse engine house – a round building with octagonal roof. The horse would have plodded round and round, turning a mechanism that drove a threshing machine. The property and the expanse of farmland and rocky coastline beyond it is only accessible by crossing the sand flats or following the narrow isthmus of the dunes. What a fabulous place to live, if a tad tricky for getting the kids to school of a morning perhaps.

By the end of our five-mile walk the puppies have slowed to my pace and flop beside me every time I pause to look at something. Good. I have tired them out for today at least. We pile in to the Landrover and drive around the north end of the island to look for some of my favourite birds – whooper swans. There is nothing quite like the audible swoosh of their wings as they power overhead.

On the way home I spy several flocks of greylag geese feeding in the fields, a hen harrier quartering some marshland and a merlin sitting on a fencepost. I'm glad to have found my binoculars at last.

~

Winter Homesteading
~ *January*

My life is getting busier with every day that passes. We now have eight sheep in our back field. Four are Texel cross and four are Leicester cross. These I am getting in exchange for some winter grazing. The barter system is alive and kicking up here. Later today three Jacob sheep are due to arrive. I asked for two but the farmer is throwing in an extra one for luck.

It is raining and raining and then snowing some. Our yard is deep in clarty mud – the kind that really sticks to your boots. Our fields are awash with water as puddles turn to ponds. We no longer have a track: we now have a river to negotiate. Despite this I need to get out and see to all these animals. Muck out the horse's stable, prepare the wee byre for the Jacob sheep, attempt to mend a leak in the turf roof of the hen house.

While I am mucking out I try to figure out a better place to put the muck heap. I need to move it out of the main yard where it is beginning to take up too much space and dominate the visual impact.

When my brother was here for New Year (a wild time in these parts – and I don't mean the weather) he suggested that it should go along the outside wall of the garden. Then the matured compost can be easily tossed over on to the vegetable patch. I need to break through a bit of fencing for this to be feasible but I agree that it is a good idea. Shifting the whole muck heap will certainly keep me busy and warm for a couple of hours.

A brief break in the interminable rain makes me want to jump on my horse for a ride to the beach. Two horse riding friends phone to say they are heading up my way, so we arrange to meet. One of the other horses is a Friesian stallion. This is one of the oldest horse breeds in Europe, indigenous to the Netherlands and traditionally used for farm and harness work.

His 16hh glossy black muscular physique is impressive and rather scary. Last time I rode out in company with him, he got a wee bit over-excited and mounted my horse - I was suddenly and frighteningly aware of having a large black leg on either side of my saddle. I'll admire his beauty from a distance today.

Home again and there is just time to shift a newly delivered tonne of coal from the yard to the byre before splashing my way down the track with two wet, muddy, bouncy pups to meet the school bus.

Shifting coal is a dismal task that inspires visions of an oil-fired heating system. A constantly warm stove to lean against and cook in and hang washing above is definitely top of my wish list.

Meanwhile I now have sheep and I have a sheepdog puppy. Something springs to mind. I'm off to see a man about a dog.

~

Storm Tides
~ *February*

When I was house hunting here last February I was initially attracted to properties right by the coast. I wanted to be able to see, hear and smell the sea from my kitchen. On hearing this, one property seller proudly announced that on stormy days the waves could come right over her house roof. Perhaps not the best sales pitch: I wasn't sure if I quite believed her, but I relegated the property to the bottom of the pile and began to look further inland.

Two days ago a combination of Spring (very high) tides and an onshore wind drove the sea to well above its usual level. From our high altitude - on this flat island a 10 metre contour is a high point – we didn't notice much difference in the sea level. However, travelling along the north coastal road to the village shop involved driving through axle-high seawater with waves hitting the Landrover at regular intervals. This delighted the boys and was a great way to identify where the Landrover is leaking (through all the doors and windows *and* the roof, as it turns out). The brilliant thing about a diesel engine is that it doesn't conk out even when driving through deep water.

Along the southern coastal road conditions were even more hair-raising. Waves crashed over the embankment, dumping seaweed, rocks and other debris onto the road and beyond, into fields and gardens. And yes, we saw the bigger waves go right over the roof of one coastal house and land in the back garden, where an inland loch was rapidly developing. Now I believe the tale. The road resembled a beach with its usual quota of fish boxes, old boots, netting and plastic bottles. We had to negotiate our way around a fifty-yard length of fencing, complete with stabs. Has anyone living south of here lost their fence recently?

The seas surrounding Orkney are moved by a complex combination of tides and currents. If you look at a map you can see why. The tides of the Atlantic Ocean to the west of mainland Britain and the North Sea to the east converge on Orkney with different timings and strengths. Further complicating this are various oceanic currents – the North Atlantic Drift, a sub-surface Mediterranean current and a Fair Isle to Orkney current - which combine to cause a complex flow of waters through the island sounds. The result can be a flattening of the tides, as all the various systems effectively cancel each other out. Or it can lead to huge tides and dangerously fast currents and tidal races.

The Churchill Barriers – causeways built to connect the southern islands with Orkney Mainland and protect the 2nd World War Fleet anchorage in Scapa Flow – cause a further twist by preventing the flow of water between west and east. Tide information for Orkney is therefore complicated. Rather than there being one high tide, often the tides will be different heights and times in different parts of the archipelago. Overall there is an almost circular flow of water around Orkney.

I realise now that even living half a mile inland, the sea can still be seen, heard and smelt. Our windows get encrusted with salt and our garden plants have to be salt tolerant. But so far we haven't had the added excitement of an ocean wave over our roof.

~

Otter
~ *February*

The dogs have just found an otter hiding behind long grass along the edge of our beach track. I think young and/or female because it is quite small - perhaps three foot from nose to tail - and I have seen much larger otters in the Hebrides, which I assume to have been adult dog otters.

When I reach the scene there is a frightful snorting noise coming from the grass and the dogs are both yelping and backing off. I realise why when I put my hand down to pull back the grass and the otter nearly has me for breakfast. What a fast mover. This may be a youngster but she is well able to defend herself against two dogs and a human. Time to back off and leave her alone.

But I digress. What I am really supposed to be doing today is planning my vegetable garden and ordering all the seeds. Thanks to my predecessors I have a large, well worked garden enclosed and sheltered by dry stone dykes and mature fuschia hedging. The proportions and layout are very much to my liking.

In front of the porch is a small amount of grass - enough to picnic on but not so large that it's a bore to mow. Beyond that is a large veggie plot, subdivided by concrete walkways just wide enough for a wheelbarrow. The southern boundary of the garden is delimited by a line of willow trees whose limbs bend elegantly in today's gentle breeze. Along the western and eastern sides are gooseberry, blackcurrant, bramble and Hebe bushes. Hearts of rhubarb nestle in the far corner. An elder tree protects the gateway.

Last autumn I dug over the veggie plot and planted a green manure - Hungarian Rye grass - to give the soil a nutrient boost and choke out the chickweed. The seed company were interested to know if it would be successful as a winter crop this far north.

Unfortunately I cannot comment on that but I can report that hens love to eat the seeds and seedlings and the chickweed. Ergo next week the hens are being fenced out of the garden.

Now it is time to decide what to grow. Tatties, onions, leeks, spinach, calabrese, beans, peas, courgettes, carrots, parsnips, a variety of salad leaves and herbs: these are the obvious crops. I will definitely plant garlic - in fact it should be in the ground already (a friend tells me that it is traditional to plant it on Christmas day). Tomatoes, peppers, aubergine, cucumber and maize will have to wait until I have created enough shelter for a polytunnel.

As I peruse my organic seed catalogue I add some more exotic plants to my shopping list. I have always wanted to grow asparagus but this takes four years to come into full production and I have never felt settled enough to grow it. Now I am settled, but will it grow this far north? Jerusalem artichoke is a root vegetable so surely it stands a chance. How about globe artichoke? I add fennel and celeriac to the list and draw the line.

Will all these crops grow here? Well, we have excellent soil and a fairly sheltered, south facing garden. But we have a short growing season, salt air and some fierce winds - a northern maritime climate. I'll let you know.

~

Downsides
~ *February*

This is tough. Friends tell me that my life here sounds too idyllic to be true and could I please tell them about the downsides quickly, before they all succumb to the temptations of paradise, jack in their jobs and move up. I have a real problem with this because I love living here, feel very at home and can't think of anything which gets me down. Nevertheless I will attempt to itemize aspects of life here which I think other people might find trying.

Most obviously there is the weather. There is nothing tame about this climate. The rain is copious, often horizontal and frequently turns into sleet, hail or snow in the winter. The wind can be fierce, cold and unrelenting. Orkney's landscape reflects this. There is a minimalist look to it – anything not very well rooted and close to the ground has blown away or failed to thrive long ago. In contrast a bout of summer sun and wind can dry out the ground incredibly quickly and cause drought conditions. This land of extremes is not to everyone's taste.

Of course to Orcadians these conditions are entirely normal, as their language reflects. What they describe as a gentle breeze is a pretty stiff gale to us Southerners (that's anyone from south of the Pentland Firth). When they talk about trees you silently substitute the term "bush".

For many people the paucity of shops could be seen as a drawback. But then again folk from the island to our north traditionally come here because our shops are so good, so it's all relative. We have three general stores, one butcher, three post offices, a knitwear outlet and a newly opened 2nd hand shop (featuring everything from antiques to zip fasteners, including kitchen sinks). We can get animal feed delivered to our doors. There is a thriving market garden. Most importantly, the stores or the hauliers will get you pretty much anything from pretty much anywhere (a bit like Harrods really).

Personally I am a fan of mail order catalogues. I have discovered that the boys can go on a virtual shopping trip, spend hours deliberating which toys or clothes they want, and then put the catalogue back in the pile and forget all about the merchandise. The ultimate in retail therapy.

There's the distance from mainland Scotland to contend with. Travelling across lumpen seas in a lurching boat or through stormy skies in a ridiculously small aircraft is not necessarily fun and involves time, expense and uncertainty. When travelling abroad most folk allow an extra day or two to get off the island, in case bad weather delays the boat and plane. It follows, therefore, that getting anywhere fast is not really an option – you are always at the mercy of the timetables of public transport (unless you have your own plane or boat I suppose) and the weather.

Life in a small community can be daunting. It is the nature of the beast that everyone knows everyone else's business. This can have positive effects (instant help if you are ill, your car breaks down or whatever) or it can descend into the negativity of gossip. In the latter case it is essential to be able to laugh, rise above, or not listen in the first place, else this is not the life for you.

~

Treb Dyke
~ February

Our house is built on a treb dyke. I know this because I have at last been to the island's library to read up on our surrounding environment. The library is within the school and I hadn't realised until quite recently that I could use it.

On my way in I spy on my three sons. Through the nursery windows I can see Fenning looking delighted at some artistic creation with blue play dough. In Class One Dale is deep in concentration, or is that just a look of utter bewilderment, as his teacher explains something.

I go in through the swing doors of the main entrance, swoon at the heat differential, smile at the Head Teacher through her glass-fronted office and head along the long and winding corridor. Suddenly aware of my muddy boots, I abandon them in the corridor and proceed in socks. Through the open door of Class Three I spy Miles in a dwam, staring wistfully out of the window. My school reports were always peppered with comments like "easily distracted" and "tends to lose concentration". Is dreaminess an inheritable characteristic?

There is a reading lesson in progress in the library, but no one seems to mind my presence. In the local information section I flick through copies of the "OrkneyInga Saga", "Orkney Nature", "The Orkney Word Book" and "Connections – Orkney and Australia" (an intriguing one, that) with half an ear on the delightful piece of local folklore being read aloud by the kids. My eye is caught by the title "Settlement in North Britain 1000 BC – AD 1000" and this is what I bring home.

Treb dykes are massive linear earthworks that run across the landscape, seemingly unrelated to today's land ownership divisions. In Norse folklore they were objects of superstition (no one seems quite sure why) and fear, being the work of the "trows" (devils or trolls). Our modern day explanation for them is that they were the land boundaries during the Bronze Age and that they were abandoned during a period of turbulent social change, which resulted in re-allocation of land.

As well as living on "The Treb" (as it is known locally) we are next to a series of settlement mounds. These are like mini "tells" – those great city mounds of the ancient Middle East – and are the result of thousands of years of occupation. Whenever a settlement is abandoned here the tendency is for it to be buried by wind-blown sand and soil.

Over the centuries, houses and byres have been built, abandoned, the ruins buried and new homes built on top. The biggest farm mound here is about twenty feet high and a couple of acres in extent. In this flat landscape that is quite a prominent bump. Thus today's farms have the look of castles, set up high on their hills with fine views over their land.

Having found all this out I feel that I am surrounded by the ghosts of thousands of past inhabitants. So far they seem friendly and I haven't knowingly met any trows. I decide to call my pottery workshop "The Treb" in recognition of its location. Phew, the development of my pottery business takes another tenuous step forward.

~

The Days
Draw Out

~ Spring
2002

Sick & Single
~ *March*

My nose is in training for the North Isles Races. My throat is as raw as the North wind. My neck glands are swollen with the effort of fighting the enemy and my ears have decided to close for the weekend. I never get ill – it's just not allowed – but I have to admit that I'm not in good fettle.

This is one of the few situations when I find it hard being a single parent. There's no one else to hold the fort, feed the children and animals, walk the dogs and light the fire (oil-fired central heating beckons). No one to mop my fevered brow, plump up my pillows, re-tune the radio or mash me a banana. In fact I can't even take to my bed because there are constantly things to do.

Miles is my Godsend. First of all he actually notices that I'm ill – how many men are that observant? Then he organises his brothers with games upstairs for the morning, leaving me to cough and sneeze in peace. He phones a friend with whom he can go swimming. We should all be going, but I cannot countenance removing my six layers of clothing to plunge into tepid waters today.

We all bundle into the Landrover and set off through the interminable rain. Having dropped Miles and his friend off at the pool I spend a cosy hour curled up in my friend's armchair while she plies me with hot drinks and jollies me along with chat. She is choked with a cold too, but she's a real stoic.

It used to horrify me to see people driving along beaches. Sacrilege! This weekend I have discovered the merits of this activity. The dogs get a run and I get to stay fairly dry and warm (given that we're in a leaky old Landrover). Fantastic. At 25mph Swan (our eight month old collie) is still keeping up with us.

We are just home and I'm stoking the fire while Dale and Fenning play chase round the kitchen table. There is a loud clatter and shriek followed by an ominous silence – the length of which gives me a pretty accurate measure of the extent of the injury.

I turn to face the scene. Fenning, not yet breathing, has blood pouring from his chin. As he catches my eye he releases his breath in a loud wail. Dale has vanished.

So just when I need to be curled up in front of my fire, we're heading back down the wet and windy road to the village to see our doctor. Fenning clutches a cloth to his chin and whimpers until Dale rallies to the cause with, "Wow Fen, look at all that blood you're making. Wicked!" at which point Fenning examines the blood-soaked cloth and begins to look rather proud of himself.

We're finally all home again. Fenning has a ster-istripped chin, a sore bum (thanks to a tetanus jab) and never wants to see a doctor again in his life. I feel like an inadequately stuffed and threadbare rag doll. Time for a hot drink before bed. The boys opt for hot chocolate. I resort to the whisky bottle. There's nothing quite like a hot toddy (or three) to cure a sore throat you know.

~

Rural Stewardship
~ *March*

More agricultural paperwork has piled up on my desk. This time it is application forms for the Rural Stewardship Scheme (RSS), which have to be submitted by the end of March. The quantity and complexity of the paperwork and the frequency of the administrative deadlines in the farming business remind me of university. It would certainly be useful to have a degree on the subject.

The RSS is the newest of a number of schemes created to encourage the adoption of environmentally friendly farming methods in Scotland. It takes over from the Environmentally Sensitive Areas (ESA) scheme and the Countryside Premium Scheme (CPS). The enduring ethos behind all of these schemes is to maintain a viable farming industry whilst enhancing the countryside for wildlife. As an ecologist who finds herself in possession of over 20 acres of farmland, I am keen to join this scheme.

But it's not so easy. As well as the main application form (13 pages) there's a form called "Prescriptions for Small Units" (7 pages) and an Environmental Audit (15 pages) to complete. The vast majority of Environmental Audits are done by professional consultants who have the expertise to identify wildlife habitats and features, map them and outline management proposals that will enhance their current conservation value. Always ready to take on a challenge (and unable to afford the consultancy fees) I'm about to attempt this myself.

I have 9.05 hectares of permanent grassland (PGRS) which means that I am eligible for the "Conservation Management Plan with Special Measures for Small Units" for which one has to have less than 10 hectares. I cannot apply for several of the management options because my land is classified as PGRS and is therefore not AAPS (Arable Aid Payments Scheme) eligible. Eligibility for this was decided back in the 1980's. Agriculture is riddled with anomalies as well as acronyms.

Having perused the 114 page glossy manual about the Rural Stewardship Scheme, I think that I can apply for up to ten of the 31 management options listed. By undertaking to restrict grazing of my grassland to certain times of year and by not cutting my hay crop until August, I can enhance my land as a wildlife habitat and attract birds such as corncrake, corn bunting and skylark. By not draining and agriculturally improving the wet grassland areas, I am providing suitable feeding and breeding grounds for lapwing, redshank, snipe, curlew and oystercatcher. Creation of field margins, conservation headlands, beetle banks, early and late vegetation cover and unharvested crops all enhance the land for wildlife. Biodiversity Action Plan (BAP) leaflets provide me with lists of prioritised habitats, animals and plants.

The next leaflet provides me with the nitty gritty – how much money I'll get per hectare for implementing these management options. Well, there has to be some incentive for making chunks of your land less productive. A farming friend tells me that her most used piece of equipment is her calculator and I can see why.

Finally, as part of an all encompassing management plan for my small unit ("croft") I will be required to get a few native breed cattle. I thought that I had drawn the line at sheep and hens, but it seems that I may yet find myself milking cows in the early hours.

Burning Rubbish
~ *March*

There is nothing quite like a wide blue sky, a bright sun and a drying wind to lift the spirits after what seems like months of rain. Within a day of this fine weather the temporary ponds are reduced to puddles, mud hardens and the fields begin to look green again. Birds sing and flit around their chosen territories. Spring is in the air.

After two or three days like this we're feeling positively euphoric. This morning the boys actually volunteer to come outside with me to feed the animals, collect the eggs and check the sheep. Miles decides that we should attack the pile of gravel heaped in the corner of the yard and spread it over the parking area. With plastic beach spades and sandcastle buckets the boys do sterling work for over two hours.

The result is an impressively smart yard – at least until the next bout of rain. Their terms are ten pence each and a trip to the shop to spend it – I wish all my bills were this reasonable. We even have lunch in the sun – chocolate spread and peanut butter sandwiches (their choice) whilst sitting in the yard admiring our work.

By afternoon the wind has dropped to an eerie calm. At intervals around the horizon we begin to notice plumes of smoke and the occasional leap of flame. Of course – a good day to burn rubbish. We gather all our boxes and papers on to the concrete hard standing outside the byres. Miles sets it alight and we stand round the blaze poking escapee boxes with long sticks until the pyre becomes a small heap of embers.

Disposal of rubbish from an island community is a perpetual problem and an expensive business. Once a week a lorry collects our bin bags and takes them on the boat to Kirkwall. On Orkney Mainland the rubbish gets baled and shipped to Shetland for incineration. The justification for our rubbish travelling so far is a bit of a mystery to me and I am trying to find out more about it. Meanwhile it makes sense to burn as much stuff as possible at home so bonfires on calm dry days are a tradition here. By the time the fire, compost bin, hens and bottle bank have been fed, there is very little which really needs to be shipped off.

As the afternoon wears on a pale haze of bonfire smoke hangs in the still air over the island. This may be deemed pollution, but it makes for a very colourful sunset. The gaudy palette of yellow ochre, burnt orange, sienna red and indigo which streaks the western sky would be hard to believe if painted on canvass.

In the early evening I drop off Miles at the pool for his Rookie Lifeguard session and Dale and Fenning with friends, then use my free hour to take the dogs for a run. I drive down a sand track with the dogs running ahead. By the time I park and walk down onto the sands it is 7pm, the sun has sunk and dusk is gathering.

A herringbone blue-grey sky, flecked with the dying orange embers of the sun, is reflected in a mirror of wet sand. Smouldering fires illuminate the village bay – the shore will be cleansed of their ashes by the midnight tide.

~

Radio Orkney
~ March

The first time I ever heard Radio Orkney I was instantly engrossed. A carpenter was explaining how he had come to design a bookcase that converts in to a coffin. His reasoning was that coffins are a terrible waste of wood, being that they just go straight in to the ground.

So from this man you can now buy a kind of made-to-measure bookcase which can fold in on itself (and around you) at the appropriate time. As well as the wood being well used for books in the interim (and with any luck long) period, once you are dead your relatives don't have to fork out for a coffin. Furthermore, not many people feel obliged to buy their coffins in advance - a bookcase is more marketable.

The interview took on the character of a Goon Show sketch with Orcadian accents. (I wonder if Spike is resting within his own bookcase now). I checked my calendar and it was nowhere near the first of April. Several months later I still have no idea whether or not the interview was sincere but I now listen to Radio Orkney regularly and there is certainly a lot of very dry humour involved.

Radio Orkney began life 25 years ago as a small outpost of the BBC. It is described as a community station: a balance of news reportage and a medium through which the community can sustain its heritage, culture and dialect. The staff of five are based in Kirkwall from where they broadcast to us every morning from 7.30 to 8.00am. After an introductory fiddle tune we get the main news and weather reports followed by a variety of local information.

On Mondays we hear about any sports events. Tuesday is devoted to the Mart Report – cow and sheep prices and any relevant agricultural news.

The Postbag is emptied and read out on Wednesdays and some fine dry humour is to be found in there. If you want a job, listen on Thursday mornings for any vacancies.

During the cold dark winter – which is considered to be the full seven months of October to April up here – Radio Orkney puts on an additional evening programme. Between the hours of 6.10 and 7pm you can hear an eclectic mix of music, chat and information. "The Bruck Programme" is filled with appeals for everything from spare parts for combine harvesters to cast off bathroom suites ("avocado" of course). Through this medium folk buy, sell and swap a plethora of goodies. "Bruck" is the Orcadian word for rubbish.

"In Conversation, Stenwick Stories" involves humorous tales from the mythical Orkney parish of Stenwick along the lines of Dylan Thomas's "Under Milkwood" (a hilarious rendition of life in a mythical Welsh mining village). The "Classic Concert" and the "Friday Request Show" give airtime to music from local to world and from every era. If you want to listen in and you are anywhere north of Golspie, just tune in to Radio Scotland at the appropriate times and you will be transported to Orkney.

I have just spoken to Dave, of Radio Orkney, and asked him about the bookcase/coffin story. It's all true and he can even give me the carpenter's name and number. I rather like the idea of being laid to rest in my very own bookcase. I hope there's room to keep the books on the shelves.

~

Salmon Galore
~ *April*

Salmon Galore in Kirkwall? When I heard the news yesterday I had to check my calendar again (there have been a lot of April Fool stories around lately). But this story is true. Last Saturday a freak combination of equinoctial tides and strong currents damaged all eight of the salmon cages at a fish farm to the Northwest of Kirkwall.

Of the astounding two hundred thousand fish involved, most were found dead in their cages. A few – a mere twenty thousand odd – escaped and swam down the coast. Having travelled some 10km these fish, probably deflected by a spur of land to the east, swam in to the confines of Kirkwall Harbour.

By Saturday afternoon Kirkwall folk became aware that their harbour was filling up with fish. A friend I spoke to said it was like looking down into an aquarium. The ensuing fishing bonanza has continued all weekend and is still going on as I write. The fishing tackle shop has been open all hours selling record quantities of landing nets, hooks and rods. Everything from spear guns to shopping trolleys is being used to try to get the fish out of the water.

A successful catch raises a cheer from the crowd. The highest catch so far is rumoured to be more than fifty salmon. The escapee fish are ready to harvest 8-10 pounders so that's a lot of salmon meat. I should think that every freezer on the island is bulging by now.

Orkney Seafarms – the owners of the fish farm – are actively encouraging the catching of these fish. That they have lost hundreds of thousands of fish is not the only problem facing the fish farm. Farmed salmon are bad news when they escape. They can potentially spread diseases and sea lice through the wild salmon and sea trout populations. If they survive to interbreed with wild salmon, they will "dilute" and weaken the species. A large proportion of the farm fish will die – they are bred in captivity and never learn to fend for themselves – and be washed on to shores and beaches.

With the best will in the world the crowd of fishers in Kirkwall Harbour will only catch a small percentage of these fish. Because farmed fish are provided with food, they have no instinctive interest in anything floating on the water's surface except fish pellets. Flies, maggots, worms and hooks hold no attraction. Consequently they are rather hard to catch.

I wonder if anyone has tried guddling. This technique involves reaching in and tickling the fish with your hands to lull it into a false sense of security before you wheech it out and throw it clear of the water. It is more of a riverine fishing technique but it might be worth a try. I haven't ever guddled (not in the fishing sense anyway) but I love the word.

The boys and I were in Kirkwall on Friday as they began their journey to visit their father for Easter. It's a shame that we missed the scene of the escapee fish by 24 hours. I'm sure we would have had great fun trying to catch ourselves some supper.

~

Spring Homesteading
~ *April*

I hereby claim three days of tee shirt and shorts weather in Orkney. I have been out gardening in nothing but the above from dawn 'til dusk. My mother sounds incredulous (and I detect gritted teeth) when she phones me from a soggy Perthshire. OK so I'll admit some goosebumps at times, but I braved it out and dug all the faster.

While my sons are away visiting their father for Easter I have organised a busy schedule for myself. My first task is to finish my application to join the Rural Stewardship Scheme, which aims to encourage farmers to adopt environmentally friendly farming practices.

In the last few weeks I have paced the marches of my ground, drawn maps and worked out a mosaic of grazed, mown and wet grassland, unharvested crops and long vegetation cover that should delight any discerning corncrake. I have discovered that my Treb Dyke is a listed Archaeological Site. This means that I must look after it – not plough it or let rabbits burrow in it or have cows poaching the ground.

I have measured the extent of my stone dykes (1000m) and my barb fences (900m). My plans include 900m of new hedge planting – along the existing stock fences – which will involve planting over 5000 hedge plants. Now I must fill in the forms, tidy up the maps and present the application to SEERAD (the Scottish Executive Environment and Rural Affairs Department). I feel like a school-girl handing in her project work.

Back at the homestead my sheep need to be shifted to a new field. I try using Swan, my collie pup. She is very excited and proud to be working. After ten minutes I'm exasperated, Swan is bewildered and the sheep are scattered across the field. We haven't quite got the hang of rounding up yet. I leave the gate open and a trough of sheep nuts in the new field. Sure enough by the next day my sheep have moved themselves through. They give me a collective haughty glance as I shut the gate.

Down in the garden I plant shallots, garlic and horseradish into freshly dug plots. The horseradish is allocated space next to the rhubarb in the far corner of the garden – it can spread like a weed. For good measure I surround it with slates dug in to the earth.

Once the sun goes down I focus my energies on the house. The 1970's swirly brown and orange stair carpet has got to go. I rip it out with a vengeance and set about stripping the wooden stairs of their old paint. After an evening of inhaling paint stripper I have such a bad headache that I decide to repaint the stairs rather than stripping and varnishing them.

The dogs get evicted to their new kennel while I paint the porch floor. In a fit of enthusiasm the walls get done too. Now I can't get out of the house and I'm due to meet a friend at the pub. I climb out of the kitchen window and hope I'll remember to go back in that way after a few beers.

All this activity is so that I don't feel too forlorn without my boys. It only partially works. I still lie awake at night hoping that they are OK.

~

Inversneuchty
~ *April*

Traffic, noise, fumes, people, endless streets of shops. I have stopped in Inverness on my way down the road to Fort William. With a 23 year old Landrover, who can just about manage 40mph going down hill with a following wind, it's been a long trip from Orkney to here and I need a break.

It is amazing how rapidly cities become scary places when one doesn't live in them. I have only been living the island life for nine months and yet I am filled with apprehension at the prospect of such trivial tasks as finding a parking space, walking through hoards of shoppers, crossing roads and keeping my bearings.

Two hours later I am laden with purchases. It's easy to identify a shopper from the islands because we buy six month supplies of everything and we're quite happy with the out of season bargain items. I have also acquired a mammoth headache: it's time to get out of town and whiz down the Loch Ness road to my friends' house, windows open, engine roaring.

I am here for a few days to see friends and meet up with my three sons – this is about half way between the Hebrides (where they are visiting their father) and our Orkney home. Getting away from home was a major task in itself. I was lucky to find friends willing to look after the dogs, cats, hens and horse. I then realised at the eleventh hour that this is a stupid time of year to be going away: four of my sheep are due to lamb. The evening before I caught the ferry I spoke to a very weary neighbouring farmer – he is in the thick of his own lambing and calving of several hundred beasts – who promised to keep an eye on my sheep for me.

The route west is a feast to my eyes. Rivers, hills, heather and woodland. It's great to see trees again, even though I would not have said that I missed them in our windswept island landscape. I see buzzards on telegraph posts, hear a woodpecker drumming vigorously and spot the silhouette of a golden eagle hanging languorously in an updraft of warm spring air.

The boys greet me in a tumble of hugs and stories, bearing gifts of pictures drawn and items collected (shells, stones, pocket-squashed sweeties, cereal packet monsters – you know the kind of thing). They tell me they love me and call me "Dad" by mistake. It's an emotionally weird transition time for all of us.

After another couple of days staying with our friends (the kids all used to go to school together in Edinburgh so they are delighted to catch up) we head up the long road to the top end of Scotland, laden with plants for our garden, heaps of shopping and several bags of dirty washing.

On the boat home I get two phone calls. One is from a friend whose job involves de-fusing landmines in war-torn countries. His lifestyle of travelling through mined war zones in armoured vehicles to organise the laborious task of clearing up the debris of war could not offer a sharper contrast to my own.

The second call is from my mother. My parents have just arrived in Orkney to find that one of our sheep appears to be in the process of producing a lamb. How quickly can we get home?

~

Bag the Bruck
~ April

One week later and we still have four pregnant sheep – and no lambs. When the weather turned cold last Monday it seemed sensible to get the sheep in. Lambs born outside in the cold or wet have only a slim chance of survival.

The shenanigans of getting them in to the stable (a lot of running about on the part of me and the boys followed by the merciful arrival of our long-suffering farmer and his dog) made us decide to keep them in until the lambs are born. So now we have four bored mums-to-be eating sheep nuts and hay and one confused horse wondering why he can't get in to his stable.

Whilst out at night to check for lamb arrivals I have also been scanning the sky. Last month I caught sight of the comet and dragged Miles out of bed to look at it. An article in the April issue of our local rag suggested we look out for a rare planetary alignment mid-month. On the 17th of April Mercury, Venus, Mars, Saturn, our moon and Jupiter were due to be lined up along the ecliptic (the apparent path of the sun through the sky) as the sun disappeared below the western horizon.

After two frustratingly cloudy twilights the 19th was clear and the planets shone obligingly. I just had to get Miles out of bed again (he's perfectly used to his mother's eccentricities) and we stood outside with binoculars until the cold air seeped into our bones. As this alignment will not happen again until August 2040, I'm glad we did.

At the weekend we were all out bagging bruck (rubbish). Orkney has an annual "Bag the Bruck" weekend, which involves collecting a winter's worth of rubbish from around the coast. The benefits are twofold: the "Bag the Bruck" outings become fundraising events and the beaches get cleaned up.

As the foot-and-mouth epidemic prevented any action last year, we now have a dismaying amount of bruck on our beaches.

We chose to go out with the Youth Club group and about twenty of us worked our way along a windswept stretch of shore. Holding the bags was the hardest job as they tried to fly like kites until we weighed them down with plastic bottles, netting, old sandshoes, cans, washing baskets – the plethora of society's detritus.

As we began to humph thirty bags of bruck up to the roadside one of the Youth Club Leaders arrived with quad bike and trailer. Once the bags were loaded all the kids jumped in too. Dale and Fenning's delighted grins could only just be seen over the sides of the trailer.

The Man from the Ministry has just called by to count my sheep. Seven out in the field, four in the stable (still no lambs). That definitely adds up to eleven. Not exactly a large flock to count so once we have done the paperwork I persuade him to take me out for a pub lunch. Well, I don't get out much you know.

~

Lambing
~ May

It's nearly midnight and I have polished off the better part of a bottle of Rioja. I used to think that drinking alone was rather sad, but now realise that with a roaring fire, a glass of wine and a good book as your companions you can guarantee a pleasant evening with no arguments.

The book of the moment is "Achilles" by Elizabeth Cook – a brilliant, brilliant retelling of his life. I am immersed in the fantastical era of the Greek Gods and Goddesses. Who needs the company of mere modern-day mortals?

Before curling up into bed I head out to walk the dogs and check the sheep. As I enter the stable (now known as the lambing shed) the bleating of a newborn lamb sends a surge of adrenaline through my body. Sure enough there's a tiny lamb attempting to stand up on its crooked little legs. My four sheep are huddled in the far corner, no one owning up to having delivered this bundle.

Then I spy the lifeless form of another lamb, flat out on the floor and still in the birthing sac. Using all the maternal skills I can muster at this late hour with my slightly fuzzy head, I pull at the sac and free the seemingly dead lamb's head. A barely discernible wheeze tells me there is a spark of life in the wee thing yet.

I wrap her in a towel and clear her nostrils of hideous quantities of slime and mucous. My stomach heaves. Then she splutters into life with a pathetic bleat. Now I feel rather proud. Cuddling her into my fleecy jacket I phone my neighbouring, long suffering and ever-patient farmer. "Help, we have lambs and I need lesson two".

I have now added lifeguard training to my list of activities. Our island swimming pool is staffed by a committed group of volunteers. Any newcomers to the island (whether they be builders, magicians, nurses, teachers, business consultants, farmers or writers) are invited, encouraged and coerced along to training sessions at an early stage. I am enjoying the physical training – it's good to get to the pool without my children and do some proper swimming. The theory is more stressful: I wince whenever I catch sight of the inch thick manual that I'm expected to wade my way through.

What with pool training sessions to attend, lambs to look after, the boys going to even more school activities and a rapidly growing garden to tame, life seems to have got a bit busy. Luckily I have visitors to put to work: my parents are here for a month and thought they might be allowed to relax and explore the island. Nope. No time for such indulgences.

The farmer comes round to look at our day old twin lambs. He rings their tails and castrates the boy (ouch). He is surprised and clearly rather envious – these are good big lambs and to get healthy twins from a ewe hog (a first timer) is doing well. Beginner's luck, obviously.

~

Cruising
~ *May*

Waves lap gently against the old stone pier as we clamber down the vertical metal ladder, faces to the wall. Fenning hesitates so I lift him away and the skipper swings him down on to the scrubbed wooden deck of the patiently waiting boat. The evening sky is as clear blue as it has been all day.

We are boarding the "Swan", a traditional Fifie fishing smack, to go for an evening sail. Launched in 1900, Swan was one of hundreds of fishing boats to work out of Shetland during the summer herring season.

There were two types of fishing boat that dominated the fleet in those days – the Fifie and the Zulu. Both were 70 to 80 foot long solidly constructed timber sailboats. The Swan is carvel built (the planks don't overlap, whereas with clinker built boats they do) in larch and pitch pine on oak. Her two masts are veritable tree trunks. She's a beauty.

In her heyday Swan, with a Whalsey crew, worked on the spring longline fishing and the driftnet herring fishing from May to September. Steamboats began to take over from sailboats, but Swan had an engine fitted which extended her useful life. By the late 1930's she was one of only five herring sailboats still working out of Shetland. Swan was finally retired in the late 1950's and began a new life as a houseboat in England.

Luckily for us she is now restored to her former glory and sailing once more in northern waters. Her summers are now spent taking school, youth or work groups on training trips, evening cruises and full-scale voyages to far off lands. You can charter her to take you to Norway, The Faroe Islands, Denmark, France, St. Kilda – pretty much wherever you want to go.

This evening is just a wee trip to enjoy the balmy sea air and to look on our island from a different perspective. We chug out from the harbour and set sail. Mainsail, foresail, mizzen sail, jib. My dim and distant knowledge of sailing is put to the test and found wanting. Mum, whose sailing days pre-date mine by several decades, has a better grasp of the subject and can tell her bowsprit from her boom, her windlass from her capstan.

We help with raising and lowering sails, winding sheets and manning the wheel, but mostly I just sunbathe and enjoy sitting still for more than two minutes. It's a great excuse to relax and do nothing.

For the kids it's an adventure of a different sort. What they will remember is the huge biscuit barrel, the ladders down to the cabins and the bunks tucked into the walls. Sailing? What sailing?

What I am avoiding back home of course is the IACS (Integrated Administration and Control System) form, otherwise known as farmers' administrative spring nightmare (amongst other, less publishable, names). It has to be in by mid May – yet another deadline. For the past few weeks I have been pushing it around my kitchen table as if it might bite me if I get too close. I guess I'll have to grasp it by the throat soon.

~

More Visitors, More Lambs
~ May

It's that time of year when friends and family from "down south" are beginning to feel like braving this northern climate to come and visit us. My parents have been here for the past month. Two evenings ago some friends from my Hebridean days arrived by yacht (having sailed round the coast of Scotland from Eigg in the Small Isles), dropped anchor in the bay closest to our house and walked up our track half an hour later. I could spot their yellow oilies a mile away.

This weekend we have friends from Dumfries camping in the garden as they indulge in a trip down memory lane – they used to live in Orkney too. Our summer holiday weeks are pretty much fully booked with visitors. This is the season when remote and beautiful island locations become an attractive holiday destination. Of course (be warned) all visitors are put to work on our various ongoing house and garden projects.

Four-year-old Fenning has decided that it is his job to look after our ten hens. Because he can't open the big gate between the garden and the hen field he runs all the way around the house and through the back field to reach the henhouse from the other direction. He then takes an egg in each hand and walks all the way back, very very carefully, to the kitchen. Yesterday there were ten eggs to collect i.e. five trips for Fenning, which took him the best part of an hour.

Our fridge is filling up with eggs despite my trawling through recipe books for variations on the omelette. We eat so many pancakes that they are no longer considered a treat and I still find myself giving eggs away to various neighbours.

At six years old, Dale is in charge of the dogs. He plays endless games of football in the yard with them – a very noisy game when dogs are involved, and we now have a veritable graveyard of punctured footballs.

Eldest boy Miles seems to have virtually left home, he has so many after school activities to attend. When he is here computer games fill his time. When I tucked him in to bed last night he asked if it would be possible to have a computer screen installed in the ceiling above his bed. I *think* he was joking.

Last week I passed one of farming's initiation tests. With instruction from my farming advisor (who was grinning from ear to ear at the time) I stuck my soaped arm up a sheep's bottom to pull out a lamb. The first one I pulled out was dead – I had naively assumed that sheep could deliver their own lambs and had left this one to her own devices for too long.

The next time I spotted a sheep in labour my mother and I tackled her to the ground and with Mum sitting on her head and me guddling around for front feet and head we eventually delivered a healthy live lamb. What a great sense of achievement. We now have five lambs (we were given an orphan lamb to put to the mother of our dead one) and no more pregnant sheep.

~

Beach Trip
~ May

It's fine weather for a swim in the ocean – if you have a wet suit. Luckily our organised visitors have brought some with them in a selection of child to adult sizes. We pile them into the Landrover along with towels, dogs and a picnic (a dangerous combination which needs policing by the children) and head for the beach we reckon will be most sheltered from the stiff north-easterly breeze.

Having squeezed into all encompassing neoprene we can plunge into the icy-cold sea and almost imagine we are somewhere more Mediterranean. I decide at once that a wetsuit is what I would like for my (rapidly approaching) 40th birthday.

While the others are ducking and diving, racing, laughing and screaming, I plonk myself next to the picnic and indulge in a little light reading. It seems appropriate, given the potential for hypothermia, cramp or being swept out to sea and drowning, that I should be reading "The Lifeguard".

This is the RLSS (Royal Life Saving Society) bible for lifeguards. It is a hefty tome, the contents of which I have to have thoroughly read and learnt by mid-June – our test date. As I read through all the possible injuries and illnesses which can befall swimmers (from broken tooth to broken neck, indigestion to heart attack) I begin to realise why lifeguards always look slightly stressed.

A slew of sand covers my manual. The dogs have found me. HotDog proudly presents me with a large white egg. It's a Fulmar egg and it's still intact and warm. I abandon my reading and walk along the dune-cliff edge until I see a likely nesting shelf.

Three Fulmars circle us and hurl abuse. Running the risk of an infuriated Fulmar hitting my head or worse still aiming her putrid peuk at me (Fulmars have a nasty habit of regurgitating revolting oily vomit at intruders) I clamber up to the empty nest and put the egg back. Now I will have to keep the dogs busy so that they don't indulge in any more inappropriate retrieving. And the boys are emerging from the sea, sleek as seals, wild eyed and exultant. My lifeguard revision will have to be put on hold.

Back at home the house fills up with salty-wet-sandy children, clothes, towels and dogs. I should really stay and help to wash, feed, bath and dry everything but luckily I have a lifeguard training session starting in ten minutes. Phew, a handy escape from domesticity.

By the time I return order has been re-established and my visitors are assembling my new bike, which arrived flat-packed last week. Given my propensity for mechanics of any description, I'm delighted to see them doing this for me.

With all the boys happily camping in the garden us grown ups contemplate the luminosity of an Orkney summer evening sky and talk about life the universe and everything over a glass of rum.

Once everyone else is asleep I sneak off for a late night whiz on my new bike. At this time of year in this land of the midnight sun I hardly even need lights.

~

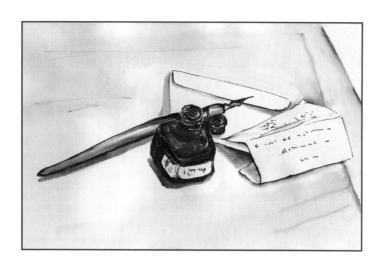

Letters
~ *May*

In among the usual weekly dose of bills, catalogues and junk mail I have received two great letters in response to this column.

In the first I read that there is a way of preserving eggs. I should have guessed that there would be. I need a tin of something called "waterglass" and a zinc bucket or crock with a lid. Fresh eggs will keep for up to nine months in a diluted solution of waterglass. So when my hens go off lay in the darkness of winter I will still have a supply of their eggs. To use these preserved eggs all I need to do is wash off the waterglass and crack them open as normal. If I want to boil them I must prick each egg with a sewing needle to avoid their shells cracking.

The second letter is from an Orcadian whose grandfather farmed at Noltland in Nortwaa' at the north end of this island. From his present urban home in Scotland he writes nostalgically of the "older and gentler rhythms" of Orkney life. He remembers Noltland tea-times when "the mackerel were barely out of the sea long enough to be gutted before they were gently poached and served with peas taken straight from the pod to the pot and gloriously floury…"Keppleton Kidney" tatties, washed on the way from the tattie-land to the stove…then drowned in Maggie Lizzie o' the Park's butter".

He goes on to speak of dairy production on the island and rues the demise of farmhouse cheese and butter making. Rising early, he and his grandfather would lead the two kye (cows) by their branks (wooden head harnesses) to the byre for milking. He describes "the texture of the old dun cow's flank against my cheek, the sound of her willingly given milk spilling into the pail, and the beautiful rich scent of that milk". Morning and suppertime porridge (made with toasted oatmeal and salt) would be lavishly covered in the creamy milk – a far cry from the pasteurised, homogenised milk of today.

To make butter there was a system of five basins set on shelves in a tall, cool, press. Each day fresh milk would be poured into a clean basin and set on the lowest shelf. This allowed the cream to rise. Cream would be skimmed off the top of each basin and added to the basin above so that the basin on the top shelf was pure cream. This was decanted into the kirn (butter churn) to make butter.

Once a week cheese was made. Milk was gently warmed on the "Enchantress" stove before adding rennet. The resulting solid mass was broken apart and drained of its whey before being "salted and put into an age-worn cheese-cog to have the last of the whey coaxed out of it over a period of days". It was stored in an "insect-proof box to let the wind and sun form a rind that would keep it for several months". Leftover milk and whey was fed to the pigs along with all the other household scraps.

These letters give me insights into Orkney life that I could never gain for myself, given my Auld Reekie roots, and some useful advice to boot. My thanks go to both writers.

~

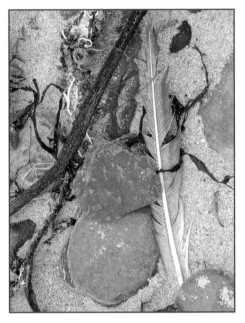

The Livin' Is Easy

~ Summer
2002

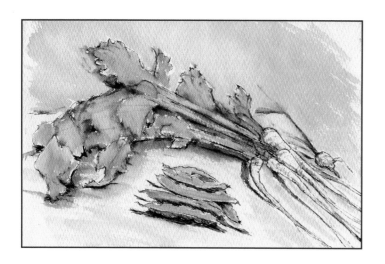

Summer Homesteading

~ *June*

In early May I spent several sweaty days digging the vegetable plot in a vain attempt to rid it of that insidious weed, the creeping buttercup. I dug deep to remove the roots then raked the clean earth to a smooth tilth.

In the byre I found old wooden planks and doors which I lugged round to the garden to use as dividers and walkways between the rows of vegetables which I could see in my mind's eye. Finally, with aching back and arms I squatted down on my hunkers, forged earth valleys with my hands and sowed my vegetable seeds.

The next step was to wait and see what might germinate. I put ten-year-old Miles in charge of the hosepipe through our spell of surprisingly dry May weather. Meanwhile, with a kind of "watched seed never germinates" feeling, I have studiously ignored the vegetable plot for the past month.

This morning I decide it is time to take a look. Lo and behold, the brown earth has grown a green mantle. I walk along my paths trying to remember what I planted in each row – I am not so organised as to have written it down. I can identify carrots, broad beans, mangetout and peas immediately. The salad plot has some very stunted looking baby lettuces, shoots of rocket and some small rounded leaves which I think might belong to the radish family.

From my parsnip seeds I can see no signs of life. Ditto the calabrese, broccoli and spinach. Of the seven courgette seeds that I planted, three have germinated. I am cosseting them under plastic beakers until they look strong enough to survive.

So that's the good news. The bad news is that the devil buttercups are back with a vengeance, aided and abetted by the appearance of a carpet of chickweed and a few sentinel thistles. In amongst the onions, shallots and garlic, which I planted back in March, are several rogue tattie plants. This was the tattie plot last year and I obviously didn't effectively clear it of old tatties. In this year's official tattie plot I can see rather a lot of grass ambushing the emerging potato plants. All in all another weeding session is required of me – pretty damn quick.

Out in our fields the sun and rain have worked wonders. The grass is high and verdant green, albeit interspersed with rather too many dockens for my liking. Down in the bottom field clumps of Iris have reached two to three feet tall and marsh marigold carpets the wetter areas. Nesting lapwing call out and flip-flop through the air from dawn 'til dusk. This rough, wet, herb-rich grassland is the perfect habitat for them.

Our lambs are looking big and fat and healthy. Chuck, the horse, is now free of his winter rug and canters around looking bright eyed and glossy coated. He has even developed a grass-belly. Summertime and the living is easy.

~

Sports
~ June

The North Isles Sports day is fast approaching. This is an annual event, now in its 53rd year. Within the archipelago of Orkney the "North Isles" refers to Sanday, Stronsay, Westray, North Ronaldsay, Papa Westray (Papay) and Eday plus a plethora of smaller isles. The first three islands take it in turns to host the event: this year it is to be held here. Special boat services contrive to get all the other islanders here for 10am.

The day begins with a dinner laid on for all the visitors. It seems to me that this might be a canny way of getting them heavy with food before the racing begins. Participants can choose from 100m, 200m, 400m, 1500m (the mile) and relay races, long jump, high jump, shot-put, football and netball. Javelin and discus are outlawed – the wind too often blows them off course. The day is rounded off with the inevitable tug-o-war before tea is served to everyone.

One of my pet hates is the phrase "I used to...". To my horror I have noticed it creeping into my vocabulary more and more in the past few years, invariably linked with sport. I used to play hockey, netball and volleyball. I used to love running 800m and 1500m track races. I used to compete in county level cross-country athletics. I used to run half marathons and even managed a full one once – the London Marathon. When I mention to the school kids here that that was in 1984 there is a confused silence – none of them were even born then.

To combat the "I used to" syndrome I am going along to the athletics practice sessions. The sports field behind the school has been sanded (to smooth out lumps and holes) rolled and re-seeded. White lines mark out a 300m running track. My first challenge is to find out if I can run round the track five times. Never mind how long it takes, can I keep running for a whole mile or will my legs or lungs protest too much?

Inter islands sports events also include swimming, football and netball. Two weekends ago Miles took the boat to Kirkwall along with his team-mates to take part in a Swimming Gala. That evening they emerged off the boat a jubilant gang, having won the cup. In retrospect I wish that I had made the effort to go along and spectate.

With this in mind we all took the excursion trip to Westray last Sunday. The Westray football kids had invited us over for a match. On a stunning sun-windy morning the boat slipped through Eday Sound, past the red sandstone cliffs of the Calf of Eday and on up to Papay. Here, much to the boys' fascination, a crane lifted one car off and one lorry on – Papay has no Ro-Ro service. Half an hour later we disembarked on to Westray and walked round the scattered houses of Pierowall bay to the football grounds.

Fenning and I picnicked, played on the swings and watched footie. Miles and Dale donned their strips, boots and shin guards and played in their teams. No cups were won or lost – it was just a friendly – but we all went home happy, tired and sun-tanned.

~

I'm in a "why oh why?" mood this week. Why oh why did I ever volunteer to train as a lifeguard? Why oh why did I ever mention to the Sport's Club that I used to be athletic? Things have come to a head this week because a) we have our mock Lifeguard exam tonight and the real thing next Wednesday and b) the North Isles Sports take place this Saturday. I would like to rather belatedly amend my column of February "Downsides" to add that in small communities one tends to end up doing things one would never dream of doing anywhere else. Mostly this is good, but not always.

Volunteering to train as a Lifeguard is definitely good - without volunteer staff we would not be able to run a swimming pool on the island. The current group of trainees includes people from the most diverse of professions: a builder, a magician, a business management consultant and a writer. Would any of us have thought of becoming lifeguards had we not been living on this small island? The 35 hours of training sessions have been good fun and have made me feel much fitter. So definitely a good thing – I just can't quite believe that I have volunteered my way into an exam situation. I hate exams!

I have reluctantly set aside my current novel to revise. The entire contents of the inch thick, A4 sized NPLQ (National Pool Lifeguard Qualification) manual has to be committed to my dodgy memory. As usual the number of acronyms involved fascinates me. Every specialist subject develops its own language.

Thus, the PSOP (Pool Safety Operating Procedures) include the NOP (Normal Operating Plan) and the EAP (Emergency Action Plan). First Aid is an attempt to PPP (Preserve Life, Prevent Deterioration, Promote Recovery). Unconscious casualties require their ABC (Airway, Breathing and Circulation) to be checked and may require CPR (Cardio Pulmonary Resuscitation). Sprains and strains need the RICE (Rest, Ice, Compression, Elevation) treatment. Epileptic seizures come in CTAAP (Clonic, Tonic, Atonic, Absences and Partial) forms.

While I'm out jogging (by no stretch of the imagination could it be called running) I test my memory. How do you tell the difference between someone having a heart attack and someone choking? Or between a diabetic and a drunk? How do you treat a nosebleed? What's the difference between a wet drowning and a dry drowning? How and why do you apply a triangular bandage? How do you get a spinally injured swimmer out of the water? My head reels while my heart pounds and my muscles ache with the effort of exertion.

Back at the manual one final abbreviation catches my eye – PTSD (Post Traumatic Stress Disorder). This is something to watch out for among staff after an emergency incident has been dealt with. But as I read through the symptoms a feeling of familiarity creeps over me. Dizziness and shaking, nausea and diarrhoea, headaches, tension and lack of sleep. I think I can claim PTSD before I have even sat the exam.

~

Fiddle Club
~ *June*

Sanday pulled out all the stops: jumped the highest, ran the fastest, threw the furthest, scored the most. The North Isles Sports day progressed from sunny to overcast to rainy, but the spirits of neither athletes nor spectators could be dampened.

At the end of a long wet and sweaty afternoon everyone piled in to the school hall for tea, sandwiches and the prizegiving. Sanday folk won no less than six of the eight available cups, shields and quaichs. The damp and gently steaming crowd clapped and cheered and stamped enough to raise the roof.

Last night, with "Sanday are the Champs" still scrawled across the whiteboard, the school hall was host to a very different occasion. As part of Orkney's annual St Magnus Festival the Scottish Chamber Orchestra (SCO) strings section came here to take part in a joint concert with the Sanday Fiddle Club. This was a fantastic opportunity for our young musicians to play alongside professionals.

To add to the enchantment of an already magical evening, the programme opened with the Premiere playing of "Six Sanday Tunes" composed by the SCO's Composer Laureate, Sir Peter Maxwell Davies. Some "Max" music was perfect for the occasion: he is both an Orkney resident and the founder of the St Magnus Festival.

Max introduced his six tunes as associated with places on the island that he thinks about when he is away. Thus "Tingly Loup" is a beach where he found a lovely fossil, while "Roos Loch" provides him with one of the joys of life as he watches the sun rise over her waters every morning. This music conjured up the calm freshness of a new dawn.

"Streamers" (the Northern Lights) was a rhythmic, rocking piece in contrast to the gentle, soothing ebb and flow of "Cata Sands". Tune five "Teeohuppo" was played entirely in pizzicato in effective mimicry of the call of the lapwing. The sixth and final tune was a veritable "Stramash" – a tumult of noise which Max described as a drunken exuberance!

The programme continued with Mozart, Britten and Dvorak. The hall was packed to the gunnels. There must have been a quarter of the island population in there, including the cricket team fresh off the pitch, farmers taking a brief break from hay cutting and a high proportion of children, most of whom were glued to their seats by this entrancing performance.

After the inevitable raffle our local band "Fitakaleerie" struck up with some cracking fiddle tunes and suddenly all those confined bodies could loosen their limbs, set free their feet and whirl their partners with abandonment. Members of the orchestra were in the thick of it, stomping and birling to their hearts' content. They couldn't leave anyway, not until the morning boat. Instead they were all staying in various island homes. I expect there were some fine hangovers today.

~

Sunny Summertime Blues
~ *July*

Shom mishtake shurely? The first day of the summer holidays and it's sunny! We throw together a picnic and head for the beach – this might be our only chance.

While the dogs chase fulmars and the boys build castles and dig moats I laze, recumbent, by the picnic. It's been a stressful week (but I passed my Lifeguarding exam – a four hour slog) and I'm distinctly lacking in energy. Tomorrow is the first day of our Fiddle Club Summer School so I may not get another chance to relax for a while.

Miles, Dale and I have elected to join this Summer School and take the opportunity of a week of being taught by three professional musicians from Manchester. As we settle in to our places in the orchestra and take a look at the music, I wonder if we have been a bit rash.

By the end of Day One I am absolutely exhausted – I have never played my fiddle for more than half an hour at a stretch and today's session has lasted five hours. I also seem to have developed some kind of dyslexia. Even the simplest of tunes leap out of the page at my barely focusing eyes in a jumble of unrecognisable notes. At my regular fiddle lesson, which happens to be this evening, my arms shake with fatigue.

To relax after the hard slog of the day the Fiddle Club has organised a beach barbecue. For a venue we choose the graceful sweep of Elsness Bay. The evening sun and a drop in the wind render the air positively balmy. Our visiting musicians, none of whom have been north of Aberdeen before, are suitably seduced by the beauty of our island.

Fortified with burgers and sausages, we play Frisbee, footie and a rudimentary version of cricket on the wet sands. The braver among us (not me) strip off and dive into the freezing ocean. Our resident fiddle tutors' twin daughters are 11 today: Mum carves up a massive cake impressively decorated with musical symbols.

As the sun dips lower (it barely goes below the horizon at this time of year) we trundle back along the sand track which splits the two beaches of the Elsness peninsula. Dale rides up front on the bonnet, blazing the trail. Fenning clambers on to my knee and takes over the steering. Miles is slumped in the back, lost in thought. Do I detect teenage hormones coursing through his ten-year-old body? I'm so tired I can hardly keep my eyes open and its only 9pm.

Once at home I have to get the boys to bed (baths, hot chocolate, stories), empty and reload the washing machine and clothes line (hope it's sunny again tomorrow), make four packed lunches ("cheese sandwiches again Mum?"), run the dogs up and down the track a few times and write this column. Just occasionally single parenthood gets me down (is that violins I hear in my mind's ear?).

~

Edible Music
~ *July*

Quavers, crochets, dotted minims, double-stops, slurs, pizzicato. Musical terms all sound deliciously edible to me – fish, pizza, quarter pounders, crisps and alcohol spring to mind. I conjured up these images at the beach barbecue on the first night of our Fiddle Club Summer School week and they have sustained me through the remaining days of arduous fiddle playing.

Summer School has turned out to be great fun, disproving my misgivings about attending. The boys have loved it and don't seem to have minded the long hours of being told to sit up, hold their fiddles up and look at the music (as opposed to out of the window or at their feet).

Our three tutors from the South are all very accomplished musicians (respectively a violin, a viola and a cello player) and also great teachers. That they managed to retain a sense of humour through a week of coaching someone as slow on the uptake as me is an accolade in itself. By the end of the week my arms have muscled up a bit and I have learnt a helluva lot.

The most valuable lesson comes in handy for the concert that we give on the final night. I have learnt how to make sure that I don't start playing before anyone else, don't make any noise during the silent bits and don't continue playing after the piece has finished. In other words I have learnt how to hide at the back of an orchestra. Does every budding musician use this technique?

The concert is, in keeping with all our Fiddle Club concerts, brilliant. The concentration of musical talent on this island never ceases to amaze me. At the core of the club are two professional musicians who have chosen to live here for the last ten years and put inordinate amounts of time and energy into teaching music and running the club whilst also raising a family of five. They can lay on a mean barbecue too. In a small and isolated community the input of such commitment, talent and sheer energy has a huge impact.

After an eclectic mix of Telemann's Don Quixote, Greig's Holberg Suite and some jazzy little numbers, the concert ends with the theme tune to Raiders of the Lost Ark.

If you have been reading my columns for a while you will know how the rest of the evening goes: a raffle, a supper (trestle tables groaning with home-made delectables) and a dance. This is the time-honoured rhyme and rhythm of our island social evenings.

~

Dubious Domesticity
~ *July*

Housework is not my forte. My ex-partner always accused me of not doing any, which I used to consider outrageous nonsense but I can now admit is not far from the truth.

I reckon that I have developed a system of cleaning which keeps us marginally the right side of squalor. I sweep the kitchen floor when levels of sand and mud interfere with the pleasure of walking around barefoot. The dogs hoover up any stray food. I clean the loo when it smells.

I'm quite good about washing – both laundry and dishes – because these chores are associated with a high sense of achievement. With a pile of freshly laundered, line-dried linen in my arms I feel quite the Domestic Goddess.

On the other hand dusting and hoovering is extraordinarily dull and only to be undertaken in extreme circumstances. In fact I gave up hoovering after seeing a newspaper cartoon depicting a harassed hooverer with the caption "I vacuum therefore I am not".

Extreme circumstances include the imminent arrival of visitors – especially when they are family. Suddenly I look around my house through their eyes and see the dust on the bookshelves, the mildew around the windows and the dark tidemark on the bath. Then the panic induced surge of adrenaline kicks in and a mad house cleaning frenzy begins.

The bendy carrots, which have happily existed at the back of the fridge for some considerable time, will now have to be evicted. The dubiously sticky sofa covers could do with a wash, and its probably time to dig out all those toast crusts from down the back. The jugs and ashets, which have languished unused for months, will soon be pressed in to service and need a good scrub.

The trick is to time the great clean up such that everything gets done and yet nothing has time to get dirty again. It's more than likely that this will involve brandishing a duster well into the night before my visitors arrive.

The particular visitors we are sprucing up for this week are my brother and his family who live in the south of France. To reach us they are taking three flights: Toulouse to London, London to Aberdeen, Aberdeen to Kirkwall. They could then have taken a ten-minute flight from Kirkwall to the field opposite our school in an eight seater Islander aircraft. But they have chosen to take the slower route, slip through the North Isles by boat and disembark on to our wee island in the summer dusk.

You might think that they will not be coming for the weather. But bear in mind that Orkney has enjoyed the highest sunshine hours in the whole of Britain since Easter and the South of France is, as I write, in a deluge of rain. Vive la différence.

~

Bloody Mary
~ *July*

To hell with the housework. We're on holiday and the sun is shining. I've decided to concentrate on the essentials of life. So we've taken the boat to Kirkwall for a spending spree.

Three hours later we struggle back to the harbour laden with goodies. A plastic beach cricket kit, a bright orange Frisbee, an elegant set of silver boule, a new football and a single use camera for each boy (inspired by a three for two special offer).

Back at home I make sure that we have good supplies of picnic food and a fridge full of Bloody Mary ingredients. I can't stand the taste of tomato juice, but mix it with lime juice, Worcestershire sauce, Tabasco, celery salt and pepper and you have a pretty zappy taste bud experience. Add vodka for that extra feel good factor.

So our house may be messy but we're well equipped for beach trips. My brother and his family are due to land at Kirkwall airport at lunchtime on Sunday and the North Isles ferry doesn't leave until 8pm.

At the last minute I decide that I can't possibly wait that long to see them. So Dale, Fenning and I head across on the Saturday evening ferry to Kirkwall (Miles is playing football on Westray again).

We haven't had time to arrange any accommodation on Orkney Mainland so we take our tent and head up the road to our friends in Evie. They already have a house full of visitors but have generously said that we can camp in their garden.

I haven't pitched a tent in ten years and have never had this particular tent out of its bag (I bought it in a half price sale just before we left Edinburgh). Add to this that I am hopelessly inept at anything remotely technical or requiring method and focus and that I'm of the "if all else fails read the instructions" school of thought.

Thank goodness for Dale who, aged six, has an insatiable thirst for learning and more practical nouse than I will ever have. He and my friends have the tent pitched in a jiffy and next morning Dale takes charge of striking camp with all the assurance of a scout leader. Phew, another thing I can delegate.

My version of child rearing revolves around the philosophy of teaching skills (not necessarily by example), encouraging exploration (i.e. "work it out for yourself because I'm clueless"), delegating tasks and promoting independence ASAP.

Sunday lunchtime. We rattle down the road to Kirkwall airport in Ozzy our especially washed Landrover. With two minutes to spare we find a window overlooking the airstrip and watch out for the arrival of the Inverness plane through the azure blue sky and scudding white clouds of our brilliant summer weather.

~

HotDog R.I.P.
~ August

Where there are farms there are rats. Where there are rats there is rat poison. HotDog was our bouncy, noisy, naughty ten-month-old pup who got her nose into everything. She was a loveable rogue. A curious toddler.

She had already eaten two of our hens, chased and caught fulmars on the beach and "worried" our sheep. She was, in truth, rapidly transforming from naughty child to rebellious teenager and I was trying to figure out how to knock some sense into her.

Yesterday she was ecstatically running like the wind along the beach. The first odd thing that Miles noticed was that she was running behind our other dog, Swan. Usually she is in the lead. Then she started coughing up alarmingly bright red blood. Had she burst a lung from running so hard? Could she be choking on a rushed beach meal of dead fish or seabird? Something was definitely not right.

This island has been without a resident vet for the last few years. For veterinary treatment you have to either take your animal to Kirkwall or wait for the Kirkwall vets' occasional trips out to the north isles. HotDog looked too ill for either of these options. Making a quick decision, I drove straight to the house of a new neighbour - I had heard on the island grapevine that he was a vet.

Luckily he was there and the rumours were correct, but unluckily he could do nothing to help HotDog. Having checked for alien objects stuck in her throat he rapidly concluded that she had probably ingested rat poison, or a poisoned carcass.

By this morning she is dead. I am wracked with guilt. Could I have done anything to keep her alive? Apparently not. Unless you catch your pet in the act of eating the poison and immediately pump their stomachs and inject them with vitamin K, they are doomed.

So today we must have a burial. Thank goodness my brother is here. He and Miles decide on a grave site then strim a path and dig a hole. With heavy hearts and tearful faces we line the grave with wildflowers and curl HotDog into her final resting-place with her favourite squeaky toy and her collar. The boys and I lose the plot entirely as my brother spades earth over her.

Death is a harsh reality for such small boys to witness. But of course they are as emotionally resilient as they are vulnerable. Soon we are discussing what we should paint on HotDog's headstone. Far from the sentimentalities flicking through my head, they come up with "ate poison" or "dead" or "gone". No confusion there then.

Late at night Swan and I walk out along the freshly strimmed path to HotDog's grave. Mist hugs the warm earth under a cool, clear indigo sky: a temperature inversion. The moon hides behind a solitary band of cloud. The North Ronaldsay lighthouse winks her warning message.

Swan paws the grave then comes to sit on my feet. She has lost her best friend and now won't let me out of her sight. HotDog: R.I.P.

~

Birthday Meal
~ *August*

Its birthday time for me (40th), wedding anniversary time for my brother and his wife (20th) and party time for all of us. There are only three eating out venues on the island and only one that I haven't tried yet. This is rather inaccurately called "The Tea Rooms". The owners (an ex Leeds and Scotland goalkeeper turned local postie, and his wife) will also serve lunches and evening meals on request.

I book a table for five and a baby sitter for four (my three sons plus their five year old cousin). The menu arrives, hand-written on a pretty greeting card, via the schoolbag delivery system, the next day. We have been asked to phone through our order one day in advance – time to dig the garden veggies and catch the lobsters. This strikes me as such a sensible system – the food ultra fresh and nothing wasted – that I can't think why other restaurants don't adopt it.

To find the Tea Rooms we park at the edge of the track and follow a flagstone path through a well-kept yet rambling garden, past a byre full of hens and in through the narrow porch of an old croft house. To our east the land slopes down to the sheltered sea inlet and massive dunes of Cata Sands.

The rooms of the restaurant could not be a more delightful surprise. A tiny, wood panelled dining room barely has space for four tables. Along the corridor there's a bathroom (yes, with old enamel bathtub) and wood panelled drawing room with comfy sofas, lots of books and an open fire. The furniture, table linens and crockery seem to have been inherited from a different era. Some grand old country house perhaps. The overall effect is a pleasing paradox of intimacy and grandeur. A sense of occasion mingles with a sense of being at home.

This is a "bring your own booze" establishment and we have come laden. A Laurent-Perrier pink champagne for starters, a copious selection of reds and whites to keep us happy through the meal and a 1962 (good year that) Armagnac to relax in the drawing room with later. The food served is fresh, locally produced and beautifully served. Our main courses are stunningly simple: four lobsters, one sirloin steak. My four companions are in raptures over the lobster. My generous cut of rare-cooked Orkney sirloin tastes truly sublime.

I ask for the opinions of my fellow diners. From my American sister-in-law I get an enigmatic "I can feel the tingle already" when we first enter the dining room. I think that means she's excited. My brother waxes lyrical about the atmosphere being bigger than the room.

His friend, a Yorkshireman, announces "bloody great view, bloody good lobster" and with reference to the wines "Very skullable, BYO, needs a refill". And from me? Well, like a truly seasoned journalist I have drunk and eaten of the best and someone else is picking up the tab. Excellent.

We walk back through the garden, now lit with low-slung fairy lights to offset the gathering dusk, and head for home after a hugely enjoyable evening.

~

Seemingly endless sunshine, scudding white clouds and fresh sea breezes. In contrast to the rest of the UK, the weather in Orkney this summer has been the stuff of childhood memories.

We have spent the school holidays frequenting our local beaches and favourite places with our visitors. We have played beach cricket, raced up sand dunes, shrieked our way into the icy ocean and indulged in sandy picnics.

When not at the beach I have, in time honoured fashion, been putting my visitors to work. A few weeks ago we received a delivery of three more flat packed bikes. I quietly stashed them in the byre and hoped the boys would not notice them until I had worked out how to assemble them. As I have said before, mechanics is not my forte, even if it only amounts to winding on a couple of pedals and straightening the handle bars. Setting the gears is the last straw.

Salvation is at hand. My brother and sister in law and their friend are of that hugely resourceful ilk who can turn their hands to anything. By the time I have made the pizza for tea they have assembled two bikes and are well on with the third. Miles triumphantly cycles round the "block" (the three mile single track road which encircles our local loch) on his new 21 gear bike.

While tinkering with the bikes my brother spies the strimmer and before I know it he's off round the garden strimming every blade of grass that dares to exceed two inches. Next to take the rap of a stressed out businessman are the fuschia hedges: they get clipped to within an inch of their lives.

On the strength of this behaviour I am thinking of setting up an escape holiday venue for high octane business folk. Would they actually pay to come here and clip my hedges for a week?

As a parent of 3 boisterous boys it has to be said that the long summer school holidays can loom rather large. What on earth shall we do for all those hours and days and weeks of free time? But this summer has whizzed by – sunshine transforms everything – and already it's time for the boys to visit their Dad before the Autumn term begins.

This time he's taking them on a trip to London, which I have to say is rather inspirational. What could offer greater contrast to their Orkney Island existence than the streets of the big smoke?

And for me it's a chance to take a break from my full-time, full-on life as a single mum.

~

Portobello
~ *August*

My sons are holidaying with their father. My dog is staying with her parents on the next-door farm. My cats and hens are being fed by one neighbour and my horse and sheep cared for by another. It's time for some time out for this single mum.

I can't quite face the crowds of Edinburgh at Festival time, so I'm staying with friends in Portobello and diving into the city for short, intense bursts of noise, bustle and entertainment. True to character, I haven't planned this trip at all. Organising the "getting away" part takes up all my resources: I've given no thought to what I want to do while away.

As a result I only get to catch up with about half the friends I would like to. Those who happen to answer their phones or happen to be in when I call. The one who knows me well enough to badger me in to an advance arrangement. And the two that I bump into in George Street whilst frittering away the house-keeping on something self-indulgent.

Portobello: beautiful port. Developed and aptly named as a seaside holiday resort for Edinburgh's wealthy in the 19th century. The wide streets, leafy crescents and handsome houses reflect those of Edinburgh's New Town but the atmosphere is in stark contrast. Sea air fills your nostrils, sand blows up onto the pavements and a laid-back friendliness pervades the slightly scruffy shops and pubs. This is "urban beach" and I immediately feel at home. I love it.

Along the seafront is an unexpectedly long sweep of sandy beach with parallel promenade. Guesthouses, hotels with beer gardens, an amusement arcade and the local swimming pool line the promenade. Dog walkers at dawn, lunchtime picnickers, tractors that rake up the litter, late night revellers: the beach is always busy. I love the isolation of our Orkney island beaches, but the ever-changing activity of the urban beach fascinates me.

I'm on a quest for some holiday indulgence and my friend has been extolling the glories of the Portobello Turkish Steam Baths. So we head down to the sea front on a sunny, breezy, balmy evening.

Inside the grand Victorian building we enter a different world. White tiles line the floors and walls and lead the eye up to a domed, midnight blue ceiling brightened with stars of orange and yellow light. Old brass handles and rails lead you through the increasingly hot and steamy rooms or back to the icy plunge pool and a series of reclining chairs. A resident masseuse works her magic in the main room and she is the best I have ever come across, even in the Turkish and Moroccan Hammams I have frequented in the past.

Steamed and pampered, we emerge two hours later to the sound of a peaceful ocean lapping onto the darkened sands. How else can we possibly end the evening but sitting on the sea wall with a poke of chips and a can of coke?

~

Gaan Hame

~ August

It's sunny so we must be back in Orkney. I hate to go on about it (tee hee) but the summer weather up here has been fantastically better than in the rest of the UK. Our trip north becomes steadily brighter and drier. We hop off the Orkney Bus next to Kirkwall's magnificent St Magnus Cathedral and bask in the evening sunshine for a few moments before heading along the flagstone streets to our B&B.

Convention notwithstanding, I decide I'd rather have the breakfast part of the deal first. We are heading for the early morning ferry home and I just can't envisage getting all of us up in time to eat. My strange request for breakfast in the evening is granted with good humour and by 8pm we are tucking into cereal, toast, orange juice and tea. We then take turns to submerge in a huge bath before sleeping the sleep of the well travelled, well fed and well washed. Definitely a B&B I will return to.

By 9am we are home and it's great to be back on our wee island and reunited with all our animals. We have saved some apples from our travelling picnic for Chuck. While the boys feed him and scratch his ears I check him over. He's in good shape except that he has managed to cast all four shoes. I'll have to encourage the blacksmith to come up to the island as soon as possible. Meanwhile the boys can have a hunt round the field for horse-shoes.

We run round the byres looking for the cats. There's a dead rat curled in the middle of the stable floor. Having banished rat poison from our property, we now have to rely on our cats to keep the rodents at bay. It looks as if they are doing their job.

We now have our two original kittens, Omelette and Storm, a new kitten called CoolCat (named in honour of our dear departed HotDog) and a big old stray which – for obvious reasons - we call OneEye. Omelette and Storm were billed as two male kittens when our neighbours gave them to us last year. On the assumption that farmers know what they're on about when it comes to sexing animals, I didn't doubt their maleness until a few weeks ago when Omelette produced a kitten. Never assume, huh!

The garden looks overgrown again already. And who's eaten all my carrot and parsnip tops and trampled the beans? It turns out that one of my sheep found her way into the veggie plot and spent a happy day there until a neighbour chased her out.

Next morning and it's Fenning's first day at school. He puts up a weak protest about getting on to the bus then sits in the back seat and won't wave goodbye to me. As I turn back to the house alone, unexpected tears fill my eyes: that's my baby off to school.

At 1.30pm when the bus delivers him home he's transformed from baby to schoolboy – two inches taller, square shouldered and with a gleam of confidence in his eyes. Do they put something in the morning milk these days?

~

Glaamsie Skies

~ Autumn
2002

Flight
~ *September*

We're standing at the edge of a smooth green field, tracking the approach of a very small plane. There's a south-easterly breeze and the pilot chooses a grass landing instead of using the single strip of tarmac available. The wind is in the wrong direction for that today. This is my second trip on the North-Isles Inter-Island Flight Service and I'm getting used to the routine.

First you have to get to the airfield in time to watch the plane land. This is about five minutes before your scheduled departure time and represents "check-in". Having parked as neatly as possible – the parking area can squeeze six cars – you and your luggage wait by the gate. That is the field gate, although I guess it could be called the departure gate...and the arrival gate. Arriving passengers emerge and walk across the field to the "gate" followed by a trolley load of the island's letters, parcels and newspapers for the day.

Next you are invited to board the eight-seater "Islander" plane. There are four rows of double seats – reminiscent of the back seat of an old Bentley – that take up the full width of the plane. For the front two rows you have to duck under the wing and clamber in behind the pilot. For the back two rows you dodge past the luggage hold.

There's a good deal of passenger interaction as we all climb over each other to reach our seats. And of course there's no problem about who wants a window seat, although the best views are to be had from the row behind the pilot from where you can also look out of the front windscreen.

We all strap in and the pilot turns round to say "hello, Stronsay next stop, then Kirkwall". As he revs up the engine and sets off across the field, we chat – everyone knows each other after all – and

catch up on the latest island news. After a quick, bumpy trundle across the field we are miraculously airborne and flying over sea, skerries, clifftops, fields of grazing cows and farm steadings. On this bright sunshiney day the north isles are on display like a colour coded map for us to study.

I crane my neck to look at the deck of dials and switches in front of the pilot. If I'm deciphering correctly, we're flying at about 700 feet above the sea and at 120 nautical knots (130mph). It certainly doesn't feel that fast. The vintage, speed, engine noise and rattle and bump of the plane all remind me of my Landrover.

Before we know it we're dropping down again and landing on Stronsay's airfield. Two folk and Stronsay's mailbags off, two folk plus luggage on and we set off into the skies again to land at Kirkwall's swanky new airport. Coming from the north isles, Kirkwall seems dauntingly built up and busy and we have to head for a beach with a picnic to recover.

My companion is heading south and catches the next flight to Inverness. My return flight is due to get me home in time to greet the boys off the school bus. But I'm about to learn a bit more about inter-island flying in these northern climes.

~

Mist
~ *September*

I watch a southbound plane take off from Kirkwall airport and diminish into a perfect blue sky. My inter-island flight is in an hour so I find a quiet corner of the airport lounge and settle in with a mug of coffee and a book.

A while later my thoughts are interrupted by the airport tanoy announcing that,

"The Inverness plane is due to fly over us in five minutes. I'll not say "arrive" because we're fairly sure it's not going to be able to land, but it's coming to have a look."

I look up, confused by this strange message. Why can't it land? Through the viewing gallery windows, where only half an hour ago I could see the runway, green fields and blue skies, I can only see white. A heavy mist has rolled in off the sea. Sure enough, the sound of a plane overhead gets first louder, then softer, as the Inverness plane circles over us then heads south again.

Now I'm in trouble. My plane is due to get me home just in time to greet the boys off the school bus. With half an hour left until departure time, the haar looks to be thickening and closing us in entirely. A fit, wiry man in his sixties is waiting for his brother to arrive on the inter-island service from North Ronaldsay. We scan the whiteness and wait.

I take a look at the other folk waiting for the wee Islander plane. A ruddy faced man in an oily boiler suit clutching a new set of drill bits. A wild-haired young woman nursing a fiddle case. A Japanese couple, fresh-faced, impeccably dressed and smiling expectantly.

The rumbling of a small plane engine can suddenly be heard overhead and the plane itself drops down onto the runway and stops abruptly right outside the terminal. Moments later pilot and passengers appear through the side door of the building. Their faces match the whiteness of the mist. The pilot glances at us, "sorry folks, I'm not going back up in that".

The North Ronaldsay brother approaches us, his leathery crofter's tan emerging through the subsiding pallor of a very bumpy plane trip. I'm suddenly aware that, with no prospect of a plane ride home, I need to get to Kirkwall harbour to catch the ferry instead. Even as I think it, the brother I have been speaking to offers me a lift. Good mind readers, these Orcadians, and generous to a fault.

There's never a dull moment in Kirkwall. As I arrive at the pier to catch my ferry, there's a large brown cow swimming across the harbour. She wades ashore at the slipway, only to charge back into the water as some men try to catch her. She then swims on up to the north side of the harbour, lands and remains warily close to the water's edge.

As the story goes, she is one of a herd of kye (that's Orcadian for cows) being loaded onto the "Buffalo Express" – the boat which transports livestock to Aberdeen. But this girl decided to alter her travel plans, jumped off the pier and swam for freedom.

~

Wetsuits
~ September

My thinly veiled request for a birthday wet suit (!) back in May, has been granted by way of a long lost cousin donating hers. Miles has also acquired one from a cousin (handy folk, cousins).

Last weekend a friend found a wetsuit source on the internet and we ordered two "shorties" for Dale and Fenning. Once these arrive we'll be all set for more oceanic adventures.

I placed the order on a Saturday. With a three to five day delivery guarantee they will surely be with us by next weekend. But take into account that we live on an island off an island off the mainland of Scotland and the guaranteed delivery date becomes slightly less relevant. When the suits don't arrive by Friday I am beginning to think up alternative recreational pursuits for the weekend ahead.

On Saturday, as we trundle along the road to the general stores, the postie flags us down and hands a large, squashy parcel through the Landrover window. After a bit of prodding and guessing, Miles rips it open. Wetsuits! We're in business.

In terms of centigrade or Fahrenheit I haven't a clue what the sea temperature is around these Orkney Islands. All I know is that I have barely dipped my toe in throughout an uncharacteristically warm summer. The few times I have taken the plunge the severe chest pains and breathlessness as my body shrinks with the shock, have meant I'm out again within seconds.

Today there's a chill wind outdoing the weakening late September sun. Jumping into the ocean seems a pretty mad notion. Putting all sensible thoughts firmly to one side we all haul on our suits and laugh at the sight of each other clad tightly in scarlet, royal blue, lemon yellow and black. Fenning decides his is a Spiderman suit and wears it constantly for the rest of the weekend.

Having squeezed my body into all this neoprene I'm boiling hot and can't wait to take the plunge. We whizz off to the nearest beach and run across the sands, happy in our madness. A few curious seals bob nearby. Wondering at these multi-coloured phenomena - or perhaps more interested in our swimming dog - they dive and surface closer and closer until they are within 10 yards.

When we first submerge there's a nasty moment or two while icy water creeps between suit and flesh. After that we feel pretty snug and swim and splash around in the sea for 20 minutes or more. Our feet and hands and heads are still frozen, but somehow with warmth at the core, the pain of the extremities is lessened. The wetsuits also give us some buoyancy: we can float and roll and somersault like men on the moon.

Enough of the water! Time to run the length of the beach and roll down the sand dunes. Our suits dry quickly and keep us warm in the evening sun. Then we head for home, a roaring fire, hot baths and tomato soup.

~

Our island's outdoor sports activities are wrapping up for the winter with some "friendlies". Over the last few weeks we have played inter Parish matches of both netball and football. By roping in people who only ever come out to play under duress once or twice a year, each of the three Parishes managed to rustle up full junior and senior teams.

Similarly, last weekend saw us playing "old versus young" matches. Within the netball teams ages ranged from 47 to 14 with an old-young cut off of 30. That put me firmly into the old team! The game was fast and fierce with a 30:14 final score in favour of us "oldies". By the time we had finished a nippy breeze had sprung up and the sun hung low in the western sky.

Up at the football pitch another match raged on into the encroaching gloom of dusk. Some nifty footwork and an impressive turn of speed from some of the "oldies" gave them a final victory of 3:0. Jumping to keep warm at the edge of the pitch, we pondered what gave age the edge in both the football and the netball teams. The youngsters definitely had more energy (there was some alarming wheezing and beetroot complexions among the older team members) and the teams were fairly matched in terms of skill. We decided to put our success down to sheer bloody-mindedness.

By the end of this hotly contested, and very vocal, football game we could hardly make out the players and were glad that the ball was white. By 8pm full headlights were necessary for the drive home. Aye, the nights are fair drawing in up in these Northern Isles.

Last Wednesday Miles was invited to join the Primary 7 hockey team to take part in a Hockey Festival in Kirkwall. This was a complete day of coaching and games organised for children from all the islands of the Orkney archipelago. Miles has been enjoying hockey at school and was keen to go, though slightly dismayed to find he was the only boy included in our island team. He was, however, much more dismayed at the thought of getting up at 6.15am in order to get the boat in to town for the day. That's still the dead of night for this budding teenager.

After a day of heavy, unremitting rain, the team returned sodden but happy. On most trips to Orkney Mainland an hour or so of shopping time is fitted in. To his delight, Miles managed to get to his favourite – The Joke Shop – and spent his money on the usual array of infuriating practical joke props.

As islanders batten down the hatches for the long winter ahead, the community diary of events fills up with indoor sports and activities. Volleyball, football, table tennis, yoga, dancing (Scottish or line), art, singing and chess are all on offer.

But the great outdoors hasn't been entirely abandoned – I see the cricketers are still out there, and of course there's always the challenge of our 100 hole (thanks to the resident rabbits) golf course.

~

Pots
~ *October*

Fourteen months after moving to the island, I am finally doing what I set out to do – throwing pots. When I first viewed our property I fell in love with the workshop more than with the house. My intention was to set up a pottery as soon as we had all settled in. Well, I guess it's taken a year of painting walls, shifting furniture, varnishing floors and digging the garden for me to feel "settled".

I am not alone in my decision to work within art in the beautiful environment of Orkney. There are an astonishing number of artists and craftspeople living here, both born and bred Orcadians and immigrants from all over the world. I'm sure they would all agree that the space and freedom of the landscapes, nature's incredible colours and the "big skies" of purest light of their Orkney surroundings are truly inspirational.

Spread across Orkney Mainland and her surrounding islands are painters, potters, sculptors, knitters, silver and goldsmiths, glass blowers, furniture makers and weavers. Orkney has a long and strong tradition of art and craft production, from the necessary furniture, clothing and crockery to the indulgence of beautiful jewellery. Design influences are a mix of traditional, contemporary, environmental and archaeological.

For instance the Orkney chairs are made of a driftwood base with woven straw forming the back, which reflects the lack of trees here. The solid chair backs have the added advantage of keeping the draughts out, which made life cosier through the windswept winters in the un-insulated croft houses.

Knitted clothing incorporates the traditional fishermen's patterns – many of which can be traced back to particular families. Jewellery keeps alive the depictions found in the carvings and engravings left by Vikings and Picts. Orkney's landscapes are reflected in paintings and tapestries, glassware and ceramics. Whenever I visit the Orkney Mainland shops and galleries I'm always impressed by the range and quality of Orkney-produced art and inspired to begin creating my own.

Back home getting started has proved difficult. My daily priorities revolve around getting boys to school, feeding animals and staving off total chaos in the house and garden. Prompted by family, friends and a head full of ideas for my pots, I have at last found some spare time for the workshop.

In the last few weeks the shelves have filled up with greenware (unfired clay), bisque (fired pots awaiting glaze) and finished, shiny, glazed pots. My workshop is constantly warmed by the kiln and cheered by the warblings of Radio Four. My head is full of designs, colours and shapes for the pots I want to make.

On the domestic front the boys are getting used to my new activity. They now know not to look in the airing cupboard for a clean towel – these have been ousted to make room for my pots to dry out before firing. They no longer ask me why my clothes are spattered with the red/brown of terracotta. Fenning has learnt that when he is delivered home by the school bus at 1.30pm he'll find me in the workshop, not the kitchen.

~

Birds

~ *October*

As I walk down through our front field to check a loose fence wire my attention is drawn by the sound of powerful wingbeats. Seven whooper swans fly low over our track, heading east.

Down in our lower field I can see a scattering of lapwings feeding in amongst the iris beds. They remind me that autumn is rapidly turning to winter and I haven't trundled around the island with my binoculars for ages.

When I do there is plenty to see. Mixed flocks of thrushes – redwing, fieldfare, blackbird and songthrush – frequent the fields and hedges. Linnets, twite, bramblings and chaffinches all feed along a strip of tatties in a roadside field. An old, unkempt garden surrounded by overgrown willow bushes hosts goldcrests and siskins, who also forage along a furrow of nettles surrounding a nearby slurry pit.

A late, lone sedge warbler lingers on near the loch just to the south of our house. He should be off to Africa by now. I am surprised by a long-eared owl sitting on a fence post. With his long ear tufts and his orange-eyed stare he looks pretty surprised to see me too. We often see short-eared owls here, but this is the first sighting of its long-eared relative.

I realise I haven't seen our local merlin for a few weeks. We usually spot her somewhere along the road below our track, working the field edges or sitting on a telegraph pole, her raptor sharp eyes trained on the grass below, waiting for a meal to saunter unwittingly by. Has she moved south for the winter?

Back home I find a blackcap and a chiffchaff in my garden. Are they new arrivals or had I just not noticed them before?

Down by the shore and in the coastal fields, among the regular redshanks and curlews, are some grey plovers, bar-tailed godwits and lots of golden plovers.

Last week a veery turned up on North Ronaldsay (the island to our north). This small American thrush is way off course, both in terms of geography and habitat (they like woodland and streams, not the barren, open landscape of an Orkney island) and I feel sorry for it. However, it attracted the usual influx of "twitchers" wanting to see such a rare visitor and tick it off on their lists.

Personally I prefer to see the indigenous birds and regular avian visitors arriving and departing in quest of their ideal feeding and breeding grounds. There is something undeniably reassuring in the rhythm of seasonal movements of geese and swans, swallows and wheatears, ducks and waders.

~

Lumpen Seas
~ October

One of the main drawbacks of island life is leaving. It's the school break and we're heading for my brother's home in the South of France. To fly four people from the northern islands of Orkney to the southern mountains of France takes four flights and a second mortgage. So we are driving down with our friend from Yorkshire.

First we have to get to mainland Scotland and this involves two ferries. Our departure day dawns wild with wind and squalls of driven rain. We are due to catch the 6pm boat to Kirkwall. However word on the island is that the weather is set to worsen and the evening boat is unlikely to run.

I rapidly shove clothes into bags and reach the school by 11am. Here I collect the boys from their classrooms, swap their school bags for holiday packs, abandon the Landrover and cadge a lift to the pier with Dale's teacher, who is off on holiday too.

The boat journey to Kirkwall isn't as bumpy as we feared. Now we have a long afternoon to fill before the departure of our overnight Kirkwall to Aberdeen ferry. The café and toy shop do well out of us.

After supper we make for the ferry terminal for 10pm check-in. But here we are told our ferry is held up by the lumpen waters between Shetland and Orkney.

With a few dozen other travellers we settle in to the small and stuffy waiting room, annoyance waning to resignation as the hours crawl by. We don't hear the thrumming of a ship's engines against the pier until 2am, by which time we are hugely grateful for our cabin.

At 4am I awake to the sound of a boy crying out with fear. We are being tossed around relentlessly by the heaving ocean. I stifle my own fears to comfort him as best I can.

By morning the captain has told us that we won't make Aberdeen until 4pm – 9 hours late! We have a long day ahead, three of us being sick whenever we raise our heads from pillows. Only Fenning proves himself a true seaman – he loves every bump and roll of the journey and even partakes of the complimentary bangers, beans and mash served at lunchtime.

At 4pm we round the corner and can see Aberdeen at last. Then the final sting in the tale: the tide is too low to enter the harbour. We finally dock at 7pm. A great start to our holiday.

~

We are driving through France on a fine and beautiful autumn day, but I'm feeling out of sorts. We have left the sea behind us at Zeebrugge in Belgium after a blissfully uneventful North Sea crossing from Hull. I am now looking with dismay at the huge landmass that we have to cross before reaching my brother's house in the South of France.

I realise my problem. I'm feeling landlocked. My eye strays to the left of the road map. There I see some small islands off the French Atlantic coast. Ile de Ré, Belle Ile, Ile d'Yeu, Ile d'Oléron. They all look invitingly small and sandy.

It's ridiculous, of course, to make such a significant detour in an already mammoth journey. By 8pm we are ascending the huge elegant arc of the suspension bridge that spans the sea between mainland France and the Ile de Ré.

The island which greets us is indeed bathed in the sun's rays. The land is a mix of wide swathes of sand, saltpan inlets, farmland, the occasional vineyard and Mediterranean type scrub. In every garden palm trees sway in the breeze and citrus bushes drip with lemons and oranges. Scatterings of whitewashed, blue-shuttered stone or clapboard cottages line the coastal hinterland.

Through an aromatic cedar wood we find "le Bois Plage en Ré" – an almost painfully picturesque village of narrow cobbled streets, tree-shaded plazas and characterfully crooked old stone houses.

Our hotel is a perfectly restored old building decorated to reflect its nautical location. Bare scrubbed floor boards, whitewashed walls, wooden sea chests, sea-green shutters. Oil paintings depict scenes of collecting sea salt from the salt pans of the island – one of the Ile de Ré's lasting industries. White sailcloths are rigged to shade the central courtyard.

After a late meal I tuck the boys into crisp white linen and we all sink into blissful sleep. The balmy sea breeze wafting through open shutters restores my sense of well being.

Next morning, plump with croissants, we head for the nearest beach. La Plage Sauvage lives up to its name with powerful Atlantic breakers pounding a steep shoreline of deep-gold coarse sand. Driftwood, huge pine cones and barbecue remnants mark the high tide line behind which a thorny dune system is protected from erosion and human intrusion by fencing.

There's a contradiction between the desertion of the beach and the regularly spaced car parks and litterbins behind it. We are here out of season: in the summer this island must be packed.

Abandoning our clothes we leap in to the ocean and yell with fear and delight as the waves throw us out again. By trial and error we learn to body surf. The rough sand is harsh on our feet and fills the pockets of the boys' swimming trunks. Salty-wet and exhilarated we drive on round the island before heading on down through Southern France.

~

Scar

~ November

We have battered our way through French, Belgian, English and Scottish storms on our way north to Orkney. Boy, am I glad to be home. This morning the sky is beguilingly clear blue and the gales have subsided to an innocent breeze. Having seen the boys off on the school bus, I decide it's high time I walked along my local beach again.

Winter is here. The leaves are off the hedges and arctic geese graze alongside sheep in the fields. The recent stormy seas have dumped great wracks of seaweed onto our beach. Turnstones and ringed plovers pick their way through the weed and pebbles and sand.

The air is bracing with cold and the tangy, salt-fish smell of seaweed fresh from the ocean. Oval indentations at the end of sweeps of smooth sand give evidence of seals body-surfing back in to the sea after their morning haul out to sunbathe.

I walk the length of the beach, on across slippery rocks and up onto the rough grassy hinterland. Here a fencing stab marks an archaeological site. Neatly painted in bright red on a peeling, yellowing white wooden board, are the words "SITE OF VIKING BOAT BURIAL". Underneath this is nailed a yellow "warning, electric fence" sign. It is a surprisingly basic acknowledgement of such a remarkable find.

This is the site of the Scar boat-burial where the skeletons of three people were found accompanied by a sword, a gilt brooch and, most famously, a whalebone plaque depicting two dragonheads. The Norse grave dates back to between 875 and 950 AD. It had remained undetected until 1991 when a fierce sea-storm lashed the coast enough to uncover the edge of the boat. I wonder how many other treasures lie as yet undetected along this shore. As

I walk along the grassy bank, I realise I am vaguely looking – for what, I'm not quite sure.

What I find is a perfect, undamaged, flat fish. We are a good 100 yards from the sea. I have to assume that a bird brought it up here to eat, although it looks entirely unharmed. When I pick it up, intending to take it home for the boys to identify, it gives a lively wriggle. Wow, it's alive!

Holding it gently between my palms I run down over smooth-ringed boulders and silver shell sand to the water's edge. As I lower my hands into the sea, the fish flips away to the sandy depths. I am truly bemused. How did a fish get all the way up a grassy banking and survive out of water until I came along?

A low winter sun blinds me on my return along the beach. Only the curlew's plaintive cry disturbs the peace. The sea is a calm, flat blue with hardly a white cap except for those marking the submerged route out to the rocky skerry of The Riv.

It's hard to believe that yesterday these seas were so treacherous as to cause two deaths in Lerwick harbour and keep the new Northlink ferry storm-bound off the coast of Shetland for 36hours. I pity both passengers and crew - I know what it's like to be stuck on a boat in a storm.

~

Rat Attack
~ *November*

Rats. These vermin are the talk of the week as the onset of winter weather brings them in to seek shelter. Rattan (Orcadian for rats) are suddenly much more obvious in and around the farmyards and byres. Lying in bed at night I can hear one scrabbling around in our wall cavities. Or it could be a "moose wi' clogs on" as my friend puts it.

Last winter I didn't see or hear a single rat at our place. I naively thought, therefore, that we didn't have any. But I have now been taught the local yardstick for assessing the extent of your rat population. If you don't see any rats on your property it means they are there in moderate numbers. When you start seeing them, you have an epidemic on your hands. While collecting eggs last week I came face to face with a smallish rat in our hen house. It glanced nonchalantly at me for a moment before trotting off, in no particular hurry, through a hole in the back wall. That sighting, coupled with the night-time bumps and scrapes, suggests I should be doing something about reducing the population.

There are various methods, neither pleasant nor particularly efficient, for killing rats. Poison is the first one that springs to mind. It is easy to lay out and effective, but has two major drawbacks. From the human perspective, dying rats tend to curl up somewhere warm – for instance behind a fireplace – to die and subsequently stink for several weeks while they decompose. From the domestic animal perspective, ingestion of rat poison (or a poisoned carcass) is fatal. With memories of our puppy's untimely death through eating rat poison, I'm reluctant to go down that route. Wildlife like owls are also put at risk.

Rat-traps are a possibility, but again there are two problems. First off, rats are actually rather clever and not particularly amenable to the invitation to walk into a break-back trap. Secondly, rat-traps are a larger, stronger version of the sprung mousetraps that give you a nasty fright if you spring them on your fingers by mistake. I'm too scared to even try to set a rat-trap.

Of course we have our byre cats. At the last count there were three adults and three kittens. The cats' corpse tally so far this month is a teal, a lapwing and two rats, all laid out lovingly at my door. I'm more sorry about the avian victims than encouraged by the vermin.

On the Hebridean farm where I used to work a professional Ratter was employed, along with his team of terriers, to keep the rat population down. I ran into him a few times, poking around the dim and dusty corners of the farm buildings. With his long thin face, piercingly suspicious eyes and ancient, frayed, grey raincoat he looked for all the world like a rat himself. It was a time consuming, but apparently effective, business.

Finally there is the direct attack approach. Over my years of life on Hebridean and Orcadian islands I have come across several farmers stabbing rats with pitchforks or taking pot shots with a gun. There was once a rat seen running along a school corridor (I'll not divulge the school's name) which was effectively despatched when the teacher squashed it behind his filing cabinet. And I have my own story of a rat in our kitchen, which we eventually cornered and knocked on the head with the aid of a cricket bat and a hockey stick. Don't try this at home, or at least not in front of the children.

~

Hoy 1
~ November

A southeasterly gale force eight mercilessly hurls icy horizontal rain at us. Frozen to the bone, we huddle together on the deck of the wee ferry. There's a cosy lounge down below, but we don't want to miss the views of Scapa Flow as we cross from Orkney Mainland to the southern island of Hoy.

Through darkening skies we can pick out the contours of all the islands that surround Orkney's famous waters of Scapa Flow. The sporadic lights of towns and villages dotted around the horizon are outshone dramatically by those of the massive oil terminal on Flotta.

Me and my buddy are off exploring for a weekend. We have chosen to visit Hoy because on the map it looks so very different from our own flat and sandy island. The massive bulk of land looming out of the darkness as we land confirms that: this is big country.

There are only two roads to navigate on our route north to Rackwick Bay, but in the rainswept darkness we manage two wrong turns, ending in muddy farmyards, before we reach our destination. Indigo hillsides merge into the blackness of stormy skies, deep peat-bog ditches edge the narrow, winding road. It's an exhilarating journey. Tucked up at last in our cosy holiday cottage we sleep to the drumming of relentless rain.

The glory of the morning is breathtaking. Winter sun shafts through remnant storm clouds and bathes Rackwick Bay in golden light. Towering vertical cliffs flank a curve of deep gold sand and huge, rosy-pink, sea-smoothed boulders. Green fields and a tumbling river fill the valley floor. The walls of this amphitheatre are the steep inclines of rich purple-brown heather clad hills.

We follow the cliff-top path to the Old Man of Hoy – the famous 450ft Old Red Sandstone sea stack which stands just south of St John's Head, the highest vertical sea-cliff in Britain. After an hour of walking we sit as close to the cliff-edge as we dare and look across to the Old Man's sparsely vegetated head and down his long, lean torso to the crashing waves at his feet.

Seabirds circle the dark red, crumbling stack, landing on impossible ledges of clinging green vegetation. Seals sing from their haul out at its base. There is a fear that the Old Man may give up his vertical stance soon and crash into the ocean. Local attitudes to this eventuality are sanguine – I recently heard of one Orcadian comment, "Aye, but he'll mak' a bonny splash when he goes".

We stay on our perch to watch the Northlink ferry sail past us to Stromness. From up here the boat seems tiny and vulnerable as she ploughs through rough seas, the tide rip visibly against her. Then we forge an inland route through the heathery hills to home, disturbing two winter-white mountain hares and many snipe on the way. We almost miss Berriedale Wood, one of Britain's most northerly native woodlands. Birch, rowan, willow and aspen trees huddle in the clefts of the hillside.

Dusk is descending as we reach our cottage. Just time for a wee dram down on the shore before total darkness engulfs us.

~

We wake late on Sunday morning with sun streaming through our Hoy holiday cottage windows. The sky is a fierce, ice blue against the peat-brown of the rugged hills. There's not a breath of wind. The perfect day for a hike up the stiff 479m ascent of Ward Hill, the summit of this hilly island of Hoy, and indeed the highest peak in the whole of Orkney.

Looking across at Ward Hill from her neighbouring hills, the Cuilags, yesterday, I could clearly see a sleeping lion. Broad at the head, a long elegant spinal plateau, narrow haunches and a dark tail. Today we decide to drive round to the reservoir at Sandy Loch and set out from there to climb the lion's left (or northern) shoulder.

We walk through wet, black peat bog and on to the deep heathery lower slopes. These hills have a trick of looking brown from a distance. Chocolate brown, auburn, mousy brown and chestnut: like shades of hair. But in close up there's a wealth of unexpected colour. Sumptuous moss carpets of deep reds and vibrant greens nestle between banks of autumn-bronzed heather. Pale mint and silver-grey lichens give life to rock surfaces. Fronds of dying bracken add dark gold and rust-orange to the palette.

A lone blue flower nods at me as I plough through a deep stretch of still-purple heather. It looks like one of the speedwell family, but my knowledge of flora is rusty and I'm surprised it's still in flower in November.

So these are the colours of the incredible Orkney landscape too: as valid as the blues and greens of the sea and sky and the pale gold of the beaches. As I climb I conjure mental images of the pots I will glaze in these vivid hues.

The hillside is suddenly, shockingly, steep. In places we need to use our hands to grasp a clump of heather for balance. We climb in silence, breathing hard. We have to stop often to catch our breaths, rest our aching leg muscles and admire the view across Hoy Sound to Stromness. The vegetation thins out to reveal pale grey rock and scree – a sub-arctic habitat that must be a botanist's haven in spring. Now we can begin to see a view ahead and as we climb the last few yards to the summit the most amazing vista unfolds.

From this high perch we can see the whole of Orkney, laid out like a contour map beneath us. We can see what a perfectly protected harbour Scapa Flow was during wartime. We can see the famous Churchill Barriers connecting the southern isles.

On this clear day we can even make out the low-lying northern isles. Mainland Scotland stands majestic to our south. Dunnet Head protrudes clearly, as does Strathy Point further west. A mountain rises high on the horizon – is that Ben Hope? I'm convinced we can see as far west as Cape Wrath, though I could be turning distant cloud into the possibility of land.

We sit on the frozen ground, eat chocolate and break chunks of ice from the glacial pools to suck and crunch. This has to be one of the most fabulous viewpoints in Scotland.

~

Rough Seas,
Home Fires

~ Winter
2002/2003

Orkney Wirds
~ December

The whaap is fendan on the sheed. Translation: the curlew is foraging in the small field. One of the most immediately noticeable manifestations of Orkney culture is the Orcadian dialect and accent.

When we first moved here the lyrical rhythm and cadence of Orcadian delighted me, but I could barely understand one word in five. Eighteen months on I can glean the majority of an Orcadian conversation, so long as the speaker is sober and we're not in a gale force eight or above.

Now I've discovered "The Orkney Dictionary", a great wee book by Margaret Flaws and Gregor Lamb. I only had to read some of the words on the front cover – pelters, fornent, yetleen, pleep, heysk, mostleens, peedie-weys, trow – to be hooked. There are some fantastic, funky words in this language, which describe things in ways that other languages just don't seem to be able to.

The other day we spotted an injured curlew feeding in a field near the road. With its broken wing it is hardly likely to survive the winter, but for the time being it can still probe the ground for food. We passed our neighbour in her car and she called it a whaap, so I was delving into the Orkney dictionary as soon as we got home. There, in amongst all the other weird and wonderful words, I found about 60 bird names and many other animal and flower names.

Some seem to be giving the animals personal names, like Tammie-norie (the puffin) and Jennie-hunder-legs (the centipede). Some give reference to the Orkney trowies (trolls or devils), hence sea sponges are trow gloves, foxgloves are trowie-girse and grass is trowie-spindle.

Many of the bird names reflect their appearance or actions. The kestrel hovering in the wind is a moosie-haak or a wind-cuffer. The aggressive great skua swooping down to hit you on the head is a bonxie. Geese chatting in the fields are kleck (barnacle geese) and quink (brent geese). An owl is a cattieface or a catawhissie. I now imagine cats whizzing through the air at night!

More often than not there is nothing to be done for injured birds but I have been lucky twice this week. In the first instance I caught sight of a sprug (sparrow) struggling to free its leg from the top strand of a barbed wire fence. I managed to get to it before it tore it's own leg off.

Later that day we had to slow down for a skoot (guillemot) which was walking along the road. It was tripping and falling over and we assumed it was injured. Then I remembered that guillemots find it very hard to take off from land – they need water.

The chances were that it had been blown inland by the storms. So I scooped up the bird in Dale's school jacket, gave it to Miles to hold and we drove down to the beach. We released it at the water's edge and watched it scoot happily out to sea.

~

Bill's Boat
~ *December*

What can you do when you miss the last plane and the last ferry to your island destination, and you're determined still to get there?

I discovered the answer to this when my buddy's attempts to fly up to Orkney from England were thwarted by flight delays. Having set off from deepest Yorkshire at 5am and reached Aberdeen by 8am, he was then airport bound for 6fi hours because of an aeroplane with a broken windscreen wiper.

Finally flying out of Aberdeen at 2.30pm there was still a marginal chance of catching the inter-island flight from Kirkwall. At any other time of year the North Isles service would wait for passengers off the Aberdeen flight. But up here in December it's getting dark by 3.30pm and these wee planes are flown by sight rather than anything more technologically sophisticated. The pilot needs at least a drop of daylight to find the islands and their airfields. So the Aberdeen flight dropped in to Kirkwall airport ten minutes after our local plane had taken off. Damn, missed it.

Over the phone we joke about chartering a boat. I have only ever known the police to do that when business is urgent. But I have reckoned without the Orkney network and my buddy's tenacity. Ten minutes later I get another phone call. The taxi driver knows a man with a boat who might just go out on a fine night like this. His phone number is painted onto his boat so it's just a question of finding it in the harbour.

Boat found, phone call successful, skipper willing, fuel gauge checked. Within half an hour they are casting off and shuffling other fishing boats (all tied up to each other) around to get themselves out. Then buddy and skipper are chugging out of the harbour in a speedy motor cruiser, heading north. After many hours of air-conditioning, the fresh, cool, sea air prompts a blast of euphoria.

As the lights of Kirkwall bay recede, silhouettes of islands, skerries and buoys stand out against the darkening horizon. The cruiser slips across Wide Firth and into the channel, Shapinsay to starboard, Galt buoy up ahead.

It's pitch black now except for the light of the radar, GPS (Global Positioning System) and depth gauge in the wheelhouse. But the skipper knows his route well. He takes a wide berth around creel buoys – it doesn't do to foul up someone's lobster creels – and threads deftly between Taing Skerry and Grass Holm on his port side and Saltness to starboard.

With the contours of Gairsay then Wyre and Egilsay appearing on the radar it's time to veer right for a northeasterly course to keep Green Holm and then Eday to port. On up through the Stronsay Firth the ebb tide turns and the sea swell of a flood tide bounces the boat around, exhilarating sea spray washing the wheelhouse and deck.

At Loth pier the skipper manoeuvres his boat briefly alongside the vertical metal ladder for my buddy to jump ashore then turns and chugs away into the night sea.

And the price of such first class travel? Well a bottle of whiskey didn't quite cover it, but, compared to the cost of a hotel room and drowning one's sorrows in Kirkwall for a night, it was great value.

~

Games Room
~ December

It's cold, cold, cold. The wind is arctic. The rain is frozen sleet. To work in my pottery workshop I wear two pairs of fleecy trousers and four woolly tops under my boilersuit. Chilblains sting my fingers and toes. It's at times like this that I question the wisdom of living on quite such a northerly island.

Despite this I have chosen Christmas presents that will keep us (or the boys anyway) out of doors. For Miles' eleventh birthday last week we bought a full archery kit. We prop the target, backed by heavy straw matting, at the far end of the yard and keep the dog shut in the house while Miles has a go.

He's delighted and turns out to be a bit of an eagle eye. Even when a blast of icy easterly wind threatens to reroute the arrow, he manages to adjust his aim and hit the target. Just needs the Robin Hood outfit now.

Our family Christmas present is becoming a major project. We have cleared the near byre of its cache of wood, boxes, old farm implements and miscellaneous rubbish. The next task is to splash some white paint on the walls and fix up some better lighting – the existing single forty watt bulb will not be adequate for the purpose. This is to be our games room, for those days when being outdoors needs to include a roof over your head and shelter from the fierce weather.

A few weeks ago a huge package arrived by courier. Over four-foot long and two-foot wide, it's too big to fit under the Christmas tree so we have left it out in the byre. This is a games table: table-top football, table tennis, air hockey, skittles, chequers, shuffle-board and pool can all be played on its many surfaces.

I am now trying to organise (hoping someone will give us) a dartboard and a basketball hoop to nail up to the end wall.

In addition to this, I'm planning that the games room can house our painting easel, the boys huge action man trucks, Fenning's enormous castle and lots of those other noisy plastic things which I long to get out of our living room.

Of course I've done all this shopping from the comfort of my fireside, a heap of mail-order catalogues gathering around my feet, phone and credit card at the ready. I have now discovered internet shopping, but until I can get my computer next to my fire I'll stick to the more old fashioned method.

~

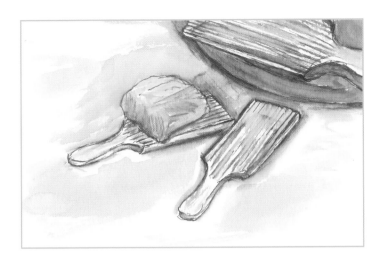

Orkney Maet
~ December

An unusually noisy cargo accompanied us on the local plane one day back in September. Behind the curtain (the basic divider between passengers and cargo) at the back of the cabin was a cardboard box full of young turkeys. At their tender age they squeaked and peeped, rather than gobbling.

I wondered, during the ten-minute flight, if they would manage to escape the box. A friend of mine once came face to face with an escapee ram (who decided he would rather be with the pilot than the luggage) during an Orkney inter-island flight.

I guess all those turkeys have enjoyed their short but free range island life by now and come to their inevitable, culinary end. However none of them found their way to our Christmas table. We are such fans of Orkney beef that we cooked up a beef Wellington instead. That's filet of Orkney beef wrapped in Nic's home-made pastry and cooked fast, to keep in all the juices.

To this we added roast tatties, parsnips, onions and garlic – all freshly dug from our garden – and lashings of gravy (fresh from a tub of gravy granules, sorry Mum, I never have learnt how to make proper gravy). Sublime.

When my brother tasted Orkney filet steak last summer he was so impressed that he likened it to Kobe beef from Japan. Kobe is an incredibly expensive delicacy - the cows are given regular massages and beer to drink during their cosseted lives, to ensure maximum tenderness of the meat.

I haven't heard of Orcadian farmers massaging their cows or buying them a pint, but whatever they are doing obviously works. The beef here is fabulous and a fraction of the price of that Japanese extravaganza.

Besides beef, Orkney produces lots of other excellent maet (food). We buy local cheese, butter, milk, ice cream and cream. Snacks and picnics are never without Orkney oatcakes and fudge (the best I have ever tasted). A lot of folk grow their own vegetables here and several market gardens sell a wide range of greens. Much to my surprise I still have lettuce and spring onion surviving in my garden, alongside the plentiful root vegetables.

A large proportion of Orkney's ebb-maet (shellfish)(velvet crabs, edible crabs, lobsters, oysters, mussels and cockles) travels south to continental Europe. But it can be bought locally too, often straight from the fishermen. I was stopped by the roadside once and invited to take my pick from a car boot full of live partan (crabs). Cockles and spoots (razorshells) are gathered from the sandy shores of Orkney when the tides are right.

In short, Orkney is a gourmet paradise.

For tonight's meal? Orkney topside, inch thick and dinner plate sized. Cooked rare then sliced into a dish of hot Worcestershire Sauce, butter, pepper corns and lemon juice. Orkney ice cream for pudding. Yum.

~

Lindisfarne
~ *January*

It's time for some festive family visits. We load up the Landrover with presents (mostly pots still warm from my kiln) and our surplus hens' eggs and set off on the morning ferry. Our trip will take in Perthshire, Stirlingshire, Edinburgh, Northumberland and Yorkshire, while for the boys there is a trip to Glasgow to see their father.

As usual when on our travels, I'm not happy unless I can visit another island. Heading south from Edinburgh down to Yorkshire gives me the perfect opportunity. Despite the fact that you can drive across a causeway to it at low tide, Lindisfarne (or Holy Island) definitely qualifies as an island and a beautiful one at that.

A few miles south of Berwick we turn east and drive down to the causeway. We've done our homework, checked the tide times and got to the crossing point with half an hour to spare. Still, the vast expanse of sand and mud flats ahead of us and the helpful sign advising us not to attempt to cross if the tide covers the road makes us a wee bit apprehensive.

The crossing is nevertheless beautiful and a breath of fresh air after several days of traffic-ridden trunk roads. On either side of the narrow causeway we can watch waders, ducks and geese moving across the sandflats. We reach Holy Island unscathed by the rising tide and the road hugs the edge of the mudflats. I get my first sighting of a flock of pale-bellied brent geese, feeding on the bright green zostera of the intertidal marsh. Bar-tailed godwits mingle with curlew in the foreground and a redshank flies right across our path. This is a bird-watcher's paradise.

Our holiday cottage is on the green, in the centre of the only village on the island. It is remarkably, almost eerily, quiet in the village and I wonder what proportion of the quaint, neatly maintained cottages are permanently lived in. Walking through Lindisfarne Priory I have strong feelings of recognition, a puzzle solved by reading some of the plethora of literature available. The monastery was founded by an Irish monk called Aidan who came here from Iona, an island I know well.

From the priory we walk down to the harbour. Upturned herring boats resemble a stranded pod of pilot whales. Some have been halved and made into storage sheds, doors built in to their severed bellies. The castle beyond perches improbably on its outcrop of hard, dark dolerite – part of the Whin Sill that runs across northern England. Down on the coast is an impressively preserved set of limekilns.

In a manner similar to Iona, once away from the village and priory one can roam the shore and extensive sand dune systems of Holy Island without seeing a soul. We stop at the Lough, a freshwater loch and reedbed, and spot dabchicks, tufted ducks, goldeneye and pochard out on the water. A coot peeks out from the bulrush and I glimpse the sleek body of something furry whipping through the long grass – a stoat?

The Links and North Shore are sandy, deserted and beautiful: I feel almost at home here.

~

First Footin

~ *January*

We're back home to a cold, clear, sunny island. New Year's day and it's perfect weather for a post-Christmas clear out of boxes, packaging, Christmas wrapping paper and newspapers. Cosy in their new fleecy jackets, the boys run between byre and bonfire site loading up the pyre. They select a long stick each to poke the burning boxes with.

While they prance around in the yard re-enacting Star Wars fights, I find more and more stuff to burn – rotten fence posts, sweepings from the garden, redundant office paperwork. I'm tempted to drag out the Christmas tree but I'm out-voted by the boys, who want to keep it in the house until the end of their school holidays.

While scanning my workshop for burnable rubbish I spot the stack of paint pots left over from our house-painting bonanza of last year. Brilliant. Our afternoon activity can be painting the now empty byre: the next stage in our mission to transform it into a games room. There's a myriad of coloured emulsion, plus a huge tub of white, to be used up.

I find a selection of old shirts and a brush for each boy and let them loose on the byre walls with the tub of white. I paint the high up bits and my buddy Nic fixes up some new lighting. We have a fresh, bright room within a couple of hours.

In the midst of all this our farm neighbours turn up to first foot us. We stop for a wee dram and they inspect our art work with bemusement: painting cow byres indeed! – what will these ferry-loupers think of next? With a, "Lang may yer lum reek" they head off to their next port of call. First footing goes on for several days up here.

All four boys go back out to tend to the dying bonfire. But I'm in the painting zone and don't want to stop. The concrete floor is next in line for a paint attack. I mix a large pot of bright blue emulsion with floor varnish – a Heath Robinson approach but it works a treat – and use the biggest brush I can find to slap it on with.

The byre is divided into cow stalls by 3ft high concrete walls and the boys have chosen a stall each as their dens. I paint Dale's stall bright blue then chuck a pot of green paint into the witch's brew. This produces a sea-green colour for Miles' stall. Finally, Fenning's stall goes emerald green. Along the centre of the byre floor is the old slurry channel. It will make a perfect bowling alley, so I paint it scarlet to brighten it up.

Reeling with a head full of paint fumes and Radio One pop music I emerge from my painting frenzy to see what the boys are up to. A fierce orange sun hangs low in the wintry sky. The embers of the bonfire have been raked under an ad hoc barbecue rig up. My nostrils fill with the aroma of sizzling sausages and steak.

Nic has revved up the storm kettle we gave him for Christmas and it's beginning to steam. Miles is carving up a loaf of bread to barbecue into toast. Fenning and Dale are hacking at my Mum's Christmas cake, guzzling chunks of marzipan and icing. We end the day with a glorious outdoor feast.

Lang may yer lum reek.

~

Cycling
~ *January*

It's one of the laws of human nature that once you have lived in a place for a while you stop noticing your surroundings. We had a friend to stay just before Christmas. As she exclaimed in wonder at the wild beauty of the island I realised that over the past months I had mostly stopped looking, stopped exploring and stopped appreciating our fantastic location.

Meanwhile back at the homestead we were clearing out the byre for painting, which involved moving our collection of no less than eight bicycles. A pang of guilt hit me as I wheeled out the swanky new touring bike that my siblings gave me for my fortieth birthday last summer. I reckon the number of times I have ridden out on it would not reach double figures. So now, with the boys back at school, I have no excuses left to delay the start of my New Year resolution – to get on my bike and explore more of this idyllic island.

We've been having some fierce frosts and today is no exception. Clad in several layers of fleecy stuff I mount my racehorse of a bike and set off down the track, cracking through ice-puddles all the way.

The tarmac road is shiny with black ice. Swan, our eighteen-month old collie, runs alongside, through the white-frosted grass of the verge. With not even a whisper of a breeze, all I can hear is the whirr of my wheels and the lonesome call of a curlew.

I've chosen a route round the northwest limb – the right wing of this dragon-shaped island. Whizzing along the road we pass sheep pawing through the frost to expose enough grass to graze, stacked mountains of pale green plastic-wrapped silage, a field of winter fodder beet. Swan cowers in the roadside ditch as a car slows past us.

We turn off the metalled road onto an initially smooth then increasingly potholed track. By the time we reach the coast the track has become a quagmire, but luckily a frozen quagmire so I can still cycle along the tractor tyre ruts. We reach the north end of Otterswick Bay, the abandoned fishing village of Ortie to our south. A milky blue sea laps lazily at the sand. A seal cranes her neck and comes in closer to check out who is disturbing her peaceful afternoon.

The rutted track gets me in the end. I'm distracted by a large splash further out in the bay, my front wheel hits a frozen lump of mud and my bike bucks me off. My left shoulder takes the brunt of the fall onto cruelly hard frozen mud and stones. Both Swan and the seal stop to stare.

Feeling a bit daft and bruised, I walk the rest of the way round the stunning beach and sand dune landscape of Whitemill Bay. The clarity of the day gives me an excellent view of North Ronaldsay, Orkney's most northerly island. Rejoining the road I cycle south, blinded by the winter sun hanging low in the sky, just in time to meet the school bus.

~

Tide Clock
~ *January*

Seven year-old Dale (with a little help from a mail order catalogue and my credit card) gave me a tide clock for Christmas. This is an ingenious device. It looks and acts like a time clock, but is actually set such that the hand rotates once every 12 hours, 25 minutes and 15 seconds. It therefore keeps pace with the "lunar day" (the time it takes for the moon to reappear at the same place in the sky) of 24 hours, 50 minutes and 30 seconds.

As the moon is the major influence over the ocean tides, this clock cleverly tells me the state of the tides. So now I can tell, before we head for a beach, whether we will be able to run across a huge expanse of sand, or have to scramble across the rocks with the sea lapping around our boots.

First we have to set the clock to coincide with our local tide times. We consult the Orcadian newspaper. But of course only the Kirkwall tide times are published: it's bound to be a bit different up here in the north isles. Nic walks Swan to the beach every morning and reports the tidal state (he measures the height of the water against rocks on the headland) on his return. Thus we calibrate the clock.

With the confidence of our new tidal knowledge we set off to walk across to the Holms of Ire, two tidal islands off the west coast. It's a breezy day – the inter-island ferry and plane services are cancelled due to the high winds and attendant choppy seas. The Landrover moves along the road like a deranged rocking horse. Fertiliser sacks and washing baskets whiz across the landscape and flap wildly from barbed wire fences. Small birds fly unnaturally, uncontrollably, fast.

We reach the crossing point and park on the peaty slope down to Whale Geo. I'm scared to leave the Landrover here lest she blows away. It takes my full body strength to open the door and I let it crash shut as soon as I have squeezed out. We are blown down to the rocks, leaning back into the wind at ridiculously impossible angles, laughing hysterically.

It's immediately obvious that we won't be able to cross to the first Holm. To the Southwest of the causeway massive waves are hurtling toward the rocks and deluging what should be a dry crossing point. Spumes of sea-foam are whisked off the wavetops and hurled across the landscape like horizontal snow. To the Northeast the sea is blown flat and races offshore as if a plug has been pulled in the ocean floor further north.

We crawl down to sea level and find a nook where a reassuringly solid wall of ancient rock shelters us from the storm. We're saturated, hair plastered to heads, skin burning with the sting of salt spray. I've optimistically packed a picnic so we hunker down to eat Orkney oatcakes, cheese, pickle and mustard – well and increasingly salted. Out comes the essential hip flask for a slug of whisky. We stare across to the Holms of Ire: have to save them up for another day.

~

Winter Dig
~ *January*

Folk who employ cleaners seem to get stressed about tidying up before their appointed cleaning day. Luckily I don't have that source of stress, but I have been feeling the same way about my garden recently. A friend who is a great gardener is due to visit next month. I want to be able to ask her for some help in the garden, but I can't possibly let her see it in its present state.

Today there's enough of a break in the storms to get out there and dig. I trundle my flat-tired, rusting wheelbarrow through the front garden of grass (can't really call it a lawn) and shrubs. The willow bushes are in bud already, with skinny limbs shooting to the skies. The concrete path to the vegetable garden is slippery with mud and dead foliage. Once through the gate I pause to survey the scene.

A surprising amount of growth has occurred in the week since I looked. Unfortunately it's all weeds. I still have a recognisable potato plot, but it is rapidly grassing over. The rows of parsnips, which we have been eating every Sunday since last September, are now reduced to one or perhaps two meal's worth.

My pea and bean plots are a cemetery of dead stems and blackened pods. The perpetual spinach is soldering bravely on, with glossy new leaf growth at the heart of each plant surrounded by the old, rotting, chewed leaves.

To avoid being overwhelmed by the enormity of the task at hand I turn my back on the larger vegetable plots and make a start on a 12ft by 6ft plot where I grew onions, shallots and garlic last year. The plot also grew a scattering of rogue tatties last season, the result of some seed potatoes left in the ground by my predecessor.

Greylag geese feed and chatter in the field next to me. My horse lazily leans his bum into the fence post between field and garden and issues contented grunts as he scratches his tail. The Inter-Island plane flies over me, heading to North Ronaldsay, and returns a while later. Storm clouds scud across an uncertain sky, but no rain falls. It's a great day to be out.

After two hours I'm hot (except for frozen feet), achy backed and grubby. My new gardening gloves came off within minutes of starting – I like to feel the soil between my fingers. I have a wheelbarrow full of rye grass, creeping buttercup (does that infuriating weed ever give up?), baby thistles and rotten tatties and onions. I also have a bucket full of tatties and onions still in perfectly good eating condition.

To my delight I dig up enough garlic heads in the final foot of ground to break up and replant two good rows. Someone will no doubt tell me that it's traditional to plant garlic on Christmas Day or possibly New Year's Day. Never mind, at least I have managed to do it before January is out.

~

Snow
~ *February*

It's 9.30am. I'm at my desk, but it's not the peaceful experience I normally enjoy. Behind me "Men in Black II" issues noisily from our video machine. Three boys' faces stare gormlessly at the screen, pyjama-clad bodies curl like caterpillars across the sofa. This is not good, not fun. This is that thing that all working parents dread – an unscheduled day off school.

This is day two of schools in Orkney being closed. Yesterday the weather was truly wild. Gale driven snow whitewashed our world. Even our cooking gas was frozen until I poured hot water along the pipe.

I did my earth mother impersonation, stoked the fire, made porridge, pancakes, pizza and flapjacks, played board games, watched a "show" enacted by the boys. At some point we ventured out into the blizzard for a snowball fight. It was a tough job just to stand up and I hung onto five year old Fenning lest he blow away entirely.

Howling gales and horizontal rain/sleet is not unusual Orkney winter weather. We are all used to hanging on to wind blown car doors. We have all developed the hunched stance required to make any headway in an Orkney "breeze". We are all prepared for rapid changes in weather conditions.

Earlier this week our high school pupils went on a day trip to Kirkwall. By evening a storm was raging and the return ferry was cancelled. So 24 kids and three teachers found themselves stranded. With a minimum of fuss the Kirkwall school hostel found food and bed space for all of them. One of the teachers bought toothbrushes and paste.

The next morning the kids were invited to join lessons at Kirkwall Grammar School, given use of the gym for a game of basketball then fed lunch before heading for their delayed boat home. When asked what they had learnt from the trip the kids' unhesitating reply was "to pack knickers and toothbrush in our schoolbags when we're on a day trip". To my mind that's a pretty good lesson for life.

A few years ago our fiddle group was invited to play on Westray, one of our neighbouring islands. They set off in their eight-seater chartered plane expecting to land in Westray within ten minutes.

Bad weather closed in rapidly, obliterating views of Westray's airfield. The pilot headed south only to find that Kirkwall, Wick, Inverness and Aberdeen airports were all closed. The wee plane eventually managed to land at Lossiemouth RAF base. The journey home took three days.

I tucked the boys into bed last night with the virtuosity of the full on Mum but secretly looking forward to getting back to my work routine today. In my dreams the boys went to school and I threw pots and wrote stories with the super-efficiency of the bionic working mother.

I woke this morning to Radio Orkney announcing school closures again. Aarrgghh.

~

Churchill Barriers
~ *February*

Wham! I instinctively shut my eyes as a wave hits the Landrover side on. Luckily I'm only the passenger and Nic seems to think it's great fun to be driving through a mischievous sea. We're crossing Churchill Barrier Number Two, notorious for rogue waves.

There are four Churchill Barriers linking the islands of South Ronaldsay, Burray, Glims Holm and Lamb Holm to Orkney Mainland. These barriers were built during World War II to effectively cut off the eastern approaches to Scapa Flow and therefore protect the British Fleet.

All four sounds were of shallow but treacherous water, with tide races of 10 to 12 knots. In an admirable feat of engineering, overhead cables were strung across the sounds between the islands. These transported and dumped rubble filled mesh containers, then massive concrete blocks. On top of all that the roadways were built – over two kilometres in total.

Scapa Flow has been appreciated as a unique natural harbour throughout human history. It is an astonishing place, surrounded by islands yet with a deep and ample flow of water and access from both west and south (and east, before the barriers were constructed) allowing passage to the open ocean in almost any wind or tide conditions.

In an effort to further protect Scapa Flow (the British Naval Fleet's main strategic base throughout both World Wars) 19 blockships were sunk across these eastern channels.

Those vessels destined to become blockships ranged from the 930 ton Reginald sunk in 1915 to the two-funnel, clipper-bowed merchant ship the Thames to the 1921 ton Empire Seaman, a German warship seized by the Brits. and scuttled in 1940. Was this a heroic or an ignominious ending for them?

With air defences, boom nets (anti-submarine steel nets that could be drawn aside to let allied ships through the passages) and coastal defence batteries to cover the other channels at Hoxa, Switha and Hoy Sounds, the Flow must have felt like a pretty safe anchorage. Unfortunately this wasn't quite the case. Six weeks into WWII a German U-boat snuk in through Holm and Kirk Sound, deftly avoiding the blockships, and torpedoed the Royal Oak, who rapidly sank taking 833 sailors with her. It was after this embarrassing and tragic disaster that the Churchill Barriers were built.

Quite apart from protecting Scapa Flow, the building of the Barriers has had several other effects. Most obviously they connect four previously isolated islands to each other and the mainland. These communities now have easy access to the Mainland for work and socialising. This has in some way compensated for the fact that the previously busy fishing ports of St Mary's and Burray have been rudely cut off from their access to the open sea.

The waves crashing over us are a reminder that the causeways have altered Orkney's already complex tidal system by preventing the flow of water between west and east. Consequently habitats have been artificially altered. Beach and dune systems have formed where there used to be open sea. Fish farmers now take advantage of the shelter to the east of the barriers.

~

Tomb of the Eagles
~ *February*

This is a bit surreal. I'm sitting in the Landrover listening to Van Morrison singing "...it was only a dream, but what a dream..." while I regard a time-warped landscape.

In my line of vision is a concrete slurry pit circa 1960's and beyond it the Liddle Bronze Age burnt mound circa 2000 to 600 BC. This is the most Southerly point of Orkney, the south end of South Ronaldsay.

I am trying to visualise life here in what is thought to have been a Bronze Age home. There are signs of living quarters, middens and burial mounds at the site. The excavated building has a flagstone floor, a large hearth set into one wall and a huge central trough. This last is a watertight construction with a one thousand-litre capacity, built of flagstone and dug into the underlying clay. Evidence suggests that this was filled with water and hot stones from the fire and used for cooking.

Personally I'd be more inclined to have a bath in the trough of hot steamy water and use the fire to cook food rather than merely heat stones. Certainly the middens are full of fire-shattered and reddened stones, so something was being heated up. Perhaps rather than a house, this was a bathing place or even a sauna.

Across a landscape of contemporary farmland and along a coastal cliff-edge path is the Isbister Neolithic chambered tomb – the famous Tomb of the Eagles – circa 3000 BC. The Isbister farmer, who excavated it himself after some twenty years of trying to get the authorities involved, discovered this astonishing site in 1958.

Bones of at least 342 people were found in the tomb, plus the remains of white-tailed sea eagles. It seems that the dead were excarnated – laid outside until their flesh was removed (most likely by the eagles) – before their bones were laid to rest within the communal tomb.

There's an ingenious go-cart and pulley system rigged up to get you along the low, tunnel entrance to the tomb. I lie stomach-down on the cart and pull myself through the tunnel, hand over hand along the rope. It's easier than it sounds. I stand up in the main chamber and look around the stalled compartments and side-cells. Human skulls stare back at me from one cell. Five thousand years dwindles to nought.

Back out in the sunlight I scan the fodder crops and grazing animals on the land. Seaspray fills my nostrils, salt-wind runs through my hair. A small fishing boat works its way back and forth through the inshore waters. Farming and fishing, earning a living from land and sea. Kitchens with flagstone floors. We might have a lot more technology to hand these days, but there hasn't been a whole heap of change here over the past 5000 years.

It's true what they say about Orkney – scratch the surface and you'll find an archaeological site. There are nearly 3000 known sites here and more being discovered all the time.

~

Italian Chapel
~ *February*

We're on our way home from our trip to South Ronaldsay, heading north across the Churchill Barriers back to Orkney Mainland. Immediately to the south of the first Barrier is the tiny island of Lamb Holm, uninhabited (I think) except for the presence of a beautiful wee church. We take the short detour to visit it.

What greets us is a surprisingly ornate front entrance with central, pillared archway flanked by decorated windows, belfry above and ornamental gothic pinnacles edging the roof. The surprise is that this is a façade, a front for the two Nissan Huts that make up the building. For this is the Italian Chapel, built by the Italian prisoners of the second world war who were captured during the North African campaign and housed here in a huddle of Nissan Huts known as Camp 60.

These several hundred POWs where brought here to help build the Churchill Barriers – a feat in itself. While they were here they used what materials they could get hold of to beautify their camp. They dug and planted a flower garden, painted screens for their theatre productions, furnished a recreation hut with a concrete billiard table, constructed a statue of St. George slaying the Dragon (a skeleton of barbed wire with concrete sculpted over it) and, finally, built this Chapel.

We enter the Chapel with a mutual sharp intake of breath. The interior is inspirational; a Nissan Hut transformed beyond belief. At the far end of the huts is the Chancel complete with altar, altar rail and Holy water stoop, all moulded out of concrete. Above the altar is a painting of the Madonna and Child, flanked by painted windows.

The whole curve of the walls and ceiling are intricately painted to represent brickwork and panelling, the sanctuary vault is frescoed with Cherubim and Seraphim, the four evangelists and the White Dove. An ornate wrought iron rood-screen sections off the Chancel. The whole interior is a fantastic work of art created by dedicated artists with minimal materials and in the face of adversity. I'm dead impressed.

Back on the road home, we have Scapa Flow to our left all the way to Kirkwall. As another legacy of the wartime activities here Scapa Flow is still littered with shipwrecks. On midsummer night of 1919 the Germans scuttled their own fleet here rather than have to hand over the 74 warships to their enemy.

Most of the ships were later salvaged. Those still on the seabed are now a mecca for scuba divers. The Konig, the Markgraf, the Brummer, the Dresden, the Coln, the Kronprinz Wilhelm, the Karlsruhe: once bristling with guns, their hulls are now encrusted with sea anemones and sponges, their cabins and engine rooms homes for fish and crabs.

At the moment the weather is too cold to contemplate digging out my dive gear to investigate these great battleships, but I might be persuadable next summer.

~

Skutherie Weet

~ Spring
2003

Several times now I have handed over the homestead reins to a trusted friend or relative while I head south for a few days. Explaining the daily routine usually runs to three or four bits of scribbled A4 paper. I have finally woken up to the idea of committing the itinerary to computer so that I can update it and print it out as necessary. Hurrah for technology. By the time I have done this it reads like the beginnings of a "Day in the Life of..." so here it is.

Seven thirty am = listen to Orkney Radio news and weather, wake the boys, let the dog out and don several layers of cosy clothing before braving the bracing Orkney climate. Head for the byres to feed all the animals.

Cats (in the hay byre): one dish full of milk, other three dishes filled with cat food mix plus meat.
Horse (in the stable): double handful of molasses chaff plus half scoop of cool mix topped with dollop of molasses, drizzle of corn oil and sprinkling of seaweed supplement. Couple of liffys of hay. Check water. Rug him up. Prop open stable door so he can go out to the back field once he's breakfasted.
Hens (in the hen house): Full scoop of hen food spread on ground outside their house. Unless it's blowing a hoolie or chucking it down in which case put the food on the hen house floor. Check water. Collect eggs. Prop door open.
Sheep (in the field): a "fling" of sheep nuts and a bale of hay if there's snow on the ground or in the run up to lambing.
Dog (in the porch): one scoop of sheepdog worker's mix plus meat, dampened. Check water dish.
Boys (somewhere in the house!): Dale (7) = self-reliant and will be in the kitchen wading through cereal. Miles (11) = needs urgent alert (from under his downie) as to the realities of time ie. his school bus is due at the track end in fifteen minutes.

Fenning (5) = leave snoring soundly – his school bus is not due for another hour.

Check through school bags for school notes requesting clean gym kit, returned library books etc. and berate the boys for not mentioning them last night. Check school timetable for fiddle, chess, piano or swimming lessons and add relevant kit to bags. Crank up the Landy and rattle and bounce down the embarrassingly potholed track to meet the bus.

Eight thirty am = drag Fenning's protesting body out of bed and lead it to the loo, then dress it and sit it in front of cereal, at which point he arrives in spirit and wades his way through 2 or 3 helpings of honey loops.

Nine am = Assemble kit-form Fenning, shoes, jacket & bag into the finished school-boy product (remembering to take a swipe at his face with the dish cloth) and once again crank up the Landy and rattle and bounce down the embarrassingly potholed track to meet the bus. Feed apple cores and carrots to the horse, who will have cantered down the field in expectation.

Nine thirty am = turn on radio 4, brew coffee, perch on kitchen counter with feet up, breath deeply.... Phew, I'll fill you in on the rest of the day when I've recovered from that bit.

~

Baked Cheesecake
~ *March*

The feast of Shrove Tuesday has to be celebrated without pancakes in our home these days. We have a constant glut of eggs from our ever-productive hens, so pancakes are our everyday fare, our staple diet, our poor-man's supper. For a rare treat with which to celebrate this festival I will have to think up an alternative. And it needs to involve eggs.

I search my cookbooks but draw a blank. I'm busy trying to recall the details of a far off child-hood culinary memory when Nic goes all psychic on me and says how about baked cheesecake? That was it!

When I was less than ten years old we used to take the long road from Scotland to Devonshire for summer holidays with family friends who lived in a rambling house near a beautiful beach cove. That's where I was given baked cheesecake so delicious that the memory has endured all these years.

The cookbooks still fail me, but the internet finds me a recipe overflowing with eggs, cream cheese, cream, biscuit and butter. Not for the faint-hearted or the figure-conscious but definitely worthy of a feast. I whizz up the thousands of calories and bake the resultant creamy gloop in the oven as instructed. It has to be left to slowly cool for many hours so I don't tell the boys it's in the oven – they would never be able to leave it alone (I'm having trouble myself).

When we finally get to take it out of the oven the cake's golden crust looks divine. Its heavenly vanilla-cream aroma takes me right back to those holidays on a hot Devonshire beach in the late 1960's. Buckets and spades, building great castles and digging deep moats. Sweaty afternoons in our friends' garden picking raspberries along bamboo corridors, hemmed in by green netting, terrified of wasps and fascinated by black hairy caterpillars.

Tea on the rolling lawn and the taste of this cake that I simply could not get enough of.

Then a guilty memory creeps in: late one afternoon my big sister and I snuk into the cool of the pantry and found the remaining half of the day's baked cheesecake nestling under a gauze hood. We ran our fingers along the cut edge and licked off the heavenly manna. Then we had to find a knife to cut off the incriminating finger marks.

Having eaten the off cuts we couldn't resist another finger-dip into the smooth creaminess of the cake. And so we repeated the process until there was so little cake left that our theft must have been outrageously obvious.

Thirty years on and this is the first time I have owned up to my misdemeanour. So this is my pre-Lenten shriving (confession and, I hope, absolution).

I'm brought back to the present moment by four clamouring boys: if I don't divide up the cake immediately I'm likely to be lynched. Such sublime food inflames the passions and I have to get the tape measure out to prove that everyone is getting their fair share. But I shouldn't be eating this Bacchanalian indulgence at all – I have a wedding dress to fit in to at the end of this month!

~

Skeetan Stanes
~ *March*

Things to learn before you're 40 (or thereabouts) should definitely include skimming stones across water. After years of throwing nice flat stones out to sea only to watch them sink without trace, I have finally mastered the art of a good skim. The technique, as I learnt a few days ago, is to throw your stone like a discus, spinning it flatly away from your body. All these years I have been throwing it like a Frisbee, in an upward arc across my body.

The next trick, which I had never really appreciated, is to pick the perfect stone. It needs to be thin and flat of course, but for that added skimability it should ideally be ever so slightly concave. Like a shallow boat or a lily pad or for that matter like the island of Tiree in the Hebrides, which mostly lies below sea level but has a coastal lip that saves it from oceanic inundation.

We came across the perfect skimming beach quite by chance the other day when walking south from Scair Tacks to Lama Ness – the tiny peninsula that offers a sheltering limb to the north-east of Otterswick Bay here on Sanday. The shore here is entirely carpeted with hand-sized, roundish, flatish stones. Please don't all rush at once.

Being a thorough researcher, I have looked up the science of skimming stones. Apparently it all relies on the stone's radius, speed and spin, the water's drag and the Earth's gravity. Your stone has to travel at a speed of at least one kilometre per hour for it to even bounce once. It has to keep spinning in order to keep bouncing because the spin prevents it from falling sideways into the water. The ideal stone would have pits across its surface – like the dimples on a golf ball – to reduce the effects of water drag. All this fascinating information comes from a French physicist called Lyderic Bocquet.

Armed with the right tools, technique and location I now have no excuses for not beating the world record holder. This is allegedly a certain Jerdone Coleman-McGhee, who made a stone bounce 38 times across the Blanco River in Texas in 1992. I have also found out (the Internet is a great thing indeed) that there is a World Stone Skimming Championship held annually on Easdale Island in Argyll.

So far I have managed 11 bounces and that was after only 20 minutes of tuition. My tutor Nic (who seems to have an endless supply of such vital life-skills and obviously skived school a lot) has a personal stone skim record of 24 bounces. We are contemplating entering this year's Championships – to be held at Easdale on Sunday 28th September.

With contestants from all around the world, it sounds like a great event. There's a section for kids as well, so we'll give the boys their first lesson this weekend, after which we'll all have to practice a lot. Yet another good reason to spend our lives on the beach.

~

Spoots & Cockles
~ March

It's a spoot tide. Spring equinox is nigh and the sea is flooding to its highest and ebbing to its lowest points on the shores of Orkney. The days are lengthening. The moon is full. In the late afternoon, when the ebb tide has exposed the sands, the boys and I don wellies and head down to one of the favoured spoot catching beaches to watch the experts at work.

Spoots are razor shells, a type of bivalve mollusc, given their nickname because of the jet of water that shoots out of the sand when they are disturbed. They burrow vertically in the sand at extreme low water level and even below the low water mark, in the shallow sublittoral. They like to be in clean sands where they filter food from the water with their siphons. If they escape their predators they can live for ten years and grow to a length of 20cm.

Unfortunately for the spoots, they are considered an Orkney delicacy. But they are tricky beasts to catch. When disturbed (by the vibration from feet on the sand surface for instance) they can retreat down through the sand at the impressive speed of 15cm per second. "Spooters" have to be fast to catch their prey.

First you have to find your spoot. The trick is to walk backwards along the water's edge at extreme low tide and watch the sand for a jet of water. There's your spoot: so drop to your knees and slice the sand with a knife until you feel it hit the spoot's shell. Then angle the knife against the shell to hold it while with your other hand you dig out the sand to expose and grasp the spoot.

As the tide turns and begins to flow the successful spooters head for home through the soft evening light with their buckets full. I have to admit now that I'm not a seafood fan, so I'm not going to try one. But I'm told that spoots fried quickly in butter make a fine feast. The onus is on speed: cooked for more than a half a minute your spoot will feel like a string of gristle in your mouth.

Going to the spoots is only a spring and (to a lesser extent) autumn equinoctial activity. The more regular seafood harvest here is that of cockles. On our way home we walk out across the slippery seaweed and rocks and onto the muddier sandflats of a good cockle beach. Cockles are found by gently raking through the sand at low tide. The characteristic chink of metal on shell will tell you if you have found cockles.

Unlike spoots they do not have a good escape system and can be quite easily collected by digging more deeply with your rake. Bucket loads are tipped into orange plastic mesh sacks and lain on the sands for a tidal wash before collection the next day. Backbreaking work, but there's a tranquillity out on the sand flats that the cocklers say they love.

~

Holmes of Ire
~ *April*

After a week of low hanging mist we wake to a clear morning. I put the washing out and our sheets flap in a droothy wind (a good drying wind) and warm spring sunshine.

Looking across to the Riv I can see that the tide is extremely low, so far out that I can make out the rocky causeway that runs the two kilometres into the ocean to the north of Whitemill Bay. I'm told that if you run you can get there and back without getting more than your feet wet, but looking at it that's hard to believe. I haven't tried it yet.

With a tide this low, today's the day for a walk across the causeways to the Holms' of Ire. We load our pockets with Orkney fudge and a bottle of water, jump in the Landy and drive out past Roos Loch. Leaving the tarmac we bump up the boggy hill south of Roos Wick, skirt past the cairn and park at Whale Point.

The route across to Inner Holm is dry as a bone, the sea well out on either side. We scramble across barnacle encrusted rocks, jumping tide pools busy with limpets, anemones and tiny crabs. Swan, our collie, runs on ahead to check out the territory then turns and hunkers down to watch our progress. In the absence of anything better, we are her flock.

Inner Holm is a half kilometre sliver of rough grassland edged with the early spring buds of campion and sea-pink and interspersed with damp patches of marsh marigold and orchids. The ruins of St. Colm's Chapel, tumble-down dry stane dykes and a row of six rounded, roofless stone wall structures are the only signs of past habitation and cultivation.

We walk around these bizarre buildings and peer over their four-foot high walls, wondering at their use. One has a makeshift gate in its side and some fishing gear stored within the shelter of its walls. The wall tops are finished off with a row of vertical stones – the same way dry stane dykes are finished here, to minimise storm damage. So it seems that they were not intended to have a roof.

The tide is on the turn so we don't hang around but carry on across the exposed rocks of Outer Sound to the next wee island, Outer Holm. This is an oval dome of land, again about half a kilometre long. As we work our way through the tussocks of grass we disturb a group of greylag geese. Rather than flying off, they circle us and land again as soon as we are past. Such territorial behaviour: are they planning to nest here?

At the farthest end of the Holms of Ire lies the mangled wreck of the steam trawler "Alex Hastie" which ran aground here in December 1940. We pick our way through the rusted hulk of metal laid out forever across the great, treacherous slabs of black rock. Even on this calm day the waves all around us are threateningly large and powerful. It's easy to see why the shores of Sanday have claimed so many ships.

~

Plantiecrues
~ *April*

Plantiecrues! After my hike across to the tidal islands of the Holms of Ire last week I determined to find out the reason for the six rounded, roofless stone wall structures built on Inner Holm. So I have discovered that they are plantiecrues: small enclosures used for growing cabbages.

Cabbage, or more accurately kail, has been grown in Scotland for at least six centuries. It's a hardy vegetable that will thrive in the worst adversities of the Scottish climate. Historically its addition to the diet could to some extent offset the widespread problem of scurvy.

The plantiecrues, or kailliecrues, were used to plant seed and grow on the young seedlings with some protection from the wind. They were built either square or round with 4 to 6ft high walls and an interior diameter averaging about 12ft. Two families could share a larger, square plantiecrue by building a low banking across the middle. This was known as a "halvers crue".

The ground inside was dug through with peat ash, clay and turf brought in from the "scattald" (the surrounding farm fields). As every good gardener knows, brassica crops are greedy on the soil's nutrients. The soil within the plantiecrues had to be replenished every other season to maintain good fertility.

Kail seed was planted in early autumn, rather bizarrely by putting it in your mouth and then spitting it out across the prepared ground. The following spring the young plants were moved out to the kailyards. The size of these was measured in terms of kail plantings. Thus a "hundersgrund" was a field into which you could plant 120 cabbages (or six score). In the "sma hunder" could be fitted five score (100) plants.

The kailyard plants were ready for eating by November, so the whole process took more than a year. Kail was originally grown for human consumption but became, and still is, a popular winter fodder for the farm animals.

Plantiecrues continue to be used as walled gardens for a variety of vegetables (including kail) and often for rhubarb. Along the coast you'll also find them storing lobster creels and other fishing gear.

Now that I have discovered plantiecrues I realise that I've seen lots of them dotted across Orkney. Such features tend to blend into the landscape to the extent that you don't question their role. I have been equally slow to query the significance of a tall round stone built tower that I look at from my kitchen window every day. I now know that it's the Mill Brae Tower, which originally housed a windmill and was subsequently used to hoist a flag to herald the arrival of cargo ships at the Kettletoft pier.

On the horizon to our south there has been a house-sized haystack ever since we moved here two years ago. Last week I stared at the horizon for ages wondering what had changed until Miles pointed out that the haystack had half gone, leaving something resembling a crooked standing stone.

~

Horses
~ *April*

A transcription of the diaries of a man called Patrick Fea of Stove, Orkney have just landed on my desk. These diaries span thirty years, from 1766 to 1796, and give a fascinating account of life on an Orkney island farm in the 18th century. It's a hefty tome and I confess that I have not read it cover to cover, but merely dipped my toes in.

The Fea family were Orkney lairds: major landowners and a part of the Orkney Islands' landed gentry. But Patrick worked the land himself, with his many farm labourers, and the diaries describe the day to day life of a hands-on farmer as well as the ongoing saga of family life. He begins every entry with a weather description. Even on the day that his wife dies, the weather notation comes first. Of course talking about the weather is one of Britain's most popular pastimes, but, for a farmer or fisherman in the northern isles, rain or sun, calm or storm has always been of paramount importance.

Reading the diary entries conjures up vivid images of farming life in the Orkney Islands. Crop sowing (oats and bere – Scottish barley) and harvesting, haymaking, raising flocks of sheep and herds of cattle: a life similar, in essence, to that of an island farmer today. Then there was dairy and vegetable production, straw-work (for ropes) using the abundant bent-grass, linen yarn spun from flax, brewing of malt ale, rabbit snaring (for fur export) and fishing. Where today's farm might employ one or two workers, Patrick Fea's 18th century farm provided work for scores of men and women, not to mention up to 50 horses.

Every aspect of the farm work involved horses, from ploughing, sowing and harvesting to transportation. Horses carted seaweed up from the beaches to fertilise the fields or for export as kelp to the glass, soap and dye industries down south. Horses collected stores from the boats, including load upon load of peat imported every summer from the neighbouring island of Eday. And of course horses were the main mode of travel - whether for riding or trap pulling.

In total Sanday is recorded as having over 850 horses in those days – more than it has people today. Patrick would regularly travel as far south as Edinburgh to buy new horses and would then spend several weeks riding, driving and boating them north. One of his three boats was large enough to accommodate seventeen horses.

Our farrier arrived to shoe my horse today so I quizzed him about horses in 21st century Orkney. He reckons there are about 80 here on Sanday and roughly one thousand in total in Orkney. Of these, there are some farm working breeds, but none actually in work. Horses here, as in the rest of Britain, are now used for recreation rather than work. But Orkney used to breed excellent work-horses and export them "sooth" i.e. to Scotland and England.

He also mentioned that he's the only commercial farrier in the whole of the Orkney Islands – and he could do with an apprentice!

~

Packing
~ *April*

Packing to go anywhere with three kids is a tricky business. Over the years I reckon I've got it down to a fine art. Three sets of clothing for each person (one set on, two sets packed) is really enough for most trips, whether they are three day or three week ones.

My sons are trained to pack their two spare sets into their backpacks along with toothbrushes, pyjamas and any toys they can fit in. The nifty rule that keeps the toy quota down is that they have to be prepared to carry their own pack.

I had trouble with Fenning on this one when we first tried it. When we reached the ferry terminal he manfully hoisted his pack onto his back and jumped out of the Landrover only to be blown over by a gust of wind. He lay on the tarmac like a turtle on its back, giggling helplessly. Centre of gravity too high.

The trip we are preparing for now is a bit different. For a start it's for six weeks so three sets of clothing might be a bit skimpy. Next I'm hoping it will involve both beach and ski bumming – we are going to a land of extremes.

Furthermore, it's going to take us a week to get there – we'll have run out of clothes before we can find a Laundromat. And finally we're going to need an entirely different set of clothes on day three of the journey because that's the day that my buddy Nic and I get married.

Seven-year-old Dale obviously thinks he's now strong enough to carry some extra items. His packing list – transcribed in his order and with his spellings - runs like this. Tedees, games, toys, pens + pencls + paper, cds + a competer, clods (I think he means clothes), cards (as in playing), top trumps,

people, wizard (the Landrover) + glob (the world globe, so we know where we're going).

Eleven-year-old Miles has a minimalist list. Surf shorts, shades, peaked cap, personal CD player and gameboy. The onus here is on "cool". Five-year-old Fenning's only requirement is that we take him straight to a place called Hot Water Beach.

According to our guide book hot water seeps through the sand here from a subterranean thermal spring. Fenning is fascinated by the concept of digging himself a bath shaped hole in the sand and languishing in the warm mineral waters. He has his yellow plastic spade and a long-saved fizzy bath bomb in his packing pile.

As for us adults, if we can get through our "to-do" list before we go, and get married without too many hitches (no pun intended), we'll be happy bunnies. And if Air New Zealand could provide some bubbly to celebrate…?

~

New Zealand North Island

~ May

The 4 millionth New Zealand citizen was born last week, amidst much publicity. New Zealand has a landmass comparable to that of the British Isles and therefore one helluva lot fewer people per square kilometre (15, as opposed to Britain's 240). Armed with these statistics we arrive in New Zealand expecting to find it as sparsely populated as our wee island back home in Orkney. With so few people and so far away from any other countries, this should surely be the ultimate in remoteness.

We fly in to Auckland (population one million, so that accounts for one quarter of the total) pre-dawn and watch the sun rise into a cloudless vibrant blue sky. Bouyant on the false energy of jet-lag we drive north through the most stunning mountainscape imaginable, precipitous ridges and jagged peaks emerging out of lavish sub-tropical vegetation. Leaving the main route we suddenly run out of tarmac and go off-roading, switchbacking up and down an alarmingly steep track canopied with deep green foliage. In a landrover this would be excellent fun but in a bulky campervan with slightly spongy brakes I'm not so sure.

Emerging from this jungle we are rewarded by the sight, far below us, of intense blue lagoon inlets, rocky islands guarding them from the wild ocean beyond. Just south of the famous Bay of Islands is an idyllic series of sandy bays with the clear blue waters, gentle surf and sand underfoot of a swimmer's paradise. All these bays are lined with houses - no chance of remoteness here. The village we stop in comprises one street of pretty, clapboard houses shaded by leafy trees, their verandahs the perfect place to relax and contemplate the sea.

At first light we're jumping into gentle surf, morning sun beginning to warm the in shore waters. As we barbeque sausages, bacon and an interesting version of toast, a man and boy emerge from the nearest house and invite us up for a cuppa. They run back up the beach at the sight of an old green and cream charabang of a school bus. The man sees his son off with a farewell Mauri war dance then whips off his tee shirt and dives into the ocean for a morning dip. Great life.

Two days later we have kitted ourselves out with some essentials - boogie boards, masks and snorkels, surf shorts, baseball caps and mirror shades. We have travelled to the most northerly point of Cape Reinga, climbed the Saharian sand dunes of Ninety Mile Beach and drunk as many blueberry smoothies as we can stomach. Our routine is arduous - jump in the sea at dawn, breakfast around the barbeque, drive on down the coast to another beach, improve our boogie boarding techniques, find a camping spot and drink a toast to the setting sun. On this basis we travel the Northland and Coromandel regions of North Island, only departing the coast after a visit to Fenning's favourite location - Hot Water Beach.

A long drive through the mountains on the high altitude Desert Road reminds us of the magnitude of this awesome country. We meet few other cars and see few signs of human habitation. Remoteness can certainly be found in New Zealand's interior. After some welcome hospitality from long lost cousins we end our North Island tour with a good dose of culture in Wellington.

Early in the morning we board the swift Lynx ferry that will take us across Cook Strait, the fast and furious stretch of water that separates the North and South Islands. We are leaving 2/3 of New Zealand's citizens behind us in the North. We will surely find some idyllic yet uninhabited coastline in the south.

~

New Zealand South Island

~ May

The ferry slows to negotiate the narrow winding channels that take us through Marlborough Sounds to Picton. On all sides tree-clad, sharp-ridged peninsulas rise sheer out of the sea. Small speed boats zip to and fro, commuting from isolated shore houses to the town by the quickest route - up through the mountains would take hours. This awesome scenery is our introduction to South Island, New Zealand.

Back on dry land we strike out along the coastal scenic route of Queen Charlotte Drive and find ourselves clinging to narrow cliff top roads through dense sub-tropical bush. When we can wrench our eyes away from the road the vista is stunning. Nelson town's cosmopolitan artiness, the deep golden beaches of Tasman Bay, the vineyards of Blenheim region; all of these we enjoy and whizz through. We're still in search of that elusive, wild, uncluttered coastline.

For a few days we slip back into our routine of sea swimming but as we travel south into Autumn the towns' heated swimming pools take on a new allure. By the time we reach the whale watching mecca of Kaikoura the weather has cut up rough and the tour boats are huddled in the harbour. Seeking solice and warmth we turn inland to the mountain-ous region of volcanic thermal springs. Within a few hours we are up to our necks in hot mineral water while the boys vent their energies on shutes and slides.

With echoes of Scotland, east coasters here would have it that it always rains on the west. But the day we drive through Lewis Pass to west coast New Zealand the sun beams at us. And here, stretching all the way down to Fiordland, are the isolated driftwood beaches we seek. The only catch is the number of other touring campervaners that have got here before us. While rejoicing at the wild beauty of these to our right we can also feast our eyes on the stupendous grandeur of the Southern Alps to our left.

Approaching Mount Cook, New Zealand's highest peak of 3754m, we yearn to head up into the ice white mountains. With neither the gear nor the time to hike through an arduous snow-scape, we opt for the easy way up the mountain and hire a helicopter. After a bird's eye view of Mount Cook and its surrounding glaciers we land on the snow above Fox Glacier for a quick snow ball fight. We're on top of the world, with nothing but a shocking ice blue sky above us and the ocean shimmering far below.

Right down south and we find out where New Zealand's 50 million sheep live. The rural landscape and the cities of Invercargill and Dunedin remind us of Scotland. The few farms not dense with sheep have herds of deer, elk, llama and alpaca.

East of Dunedin the Otago peninsula wows us with its wild rugged landscape and plethora of wildlife. We spend a mesmeric morning watching royal albatross parents fly in to feed their massive chicks. Rare yellow-eyed penguins and boisterous fur seals inhabit remote beaches and unlikely cliff faces.

It's time to hand in the camper van and fly north. And, the freedom of camping notwithstanding, it's definitely time for some luxury. We fly to Auckland and head for her largest, most indulgent hotel. As the sun sets we are in a roof-top, heated pool over-looking Auckland harbour and cracking a bottle of champagne.

~

Great Barrier Island
~ May

The boys and I walk across warm tarmac and climb aboard the familiar 8 seater inter-islander plane. It's full today and Dale gets to sit in the 'ninth' seat: next to the pilot. His eyes widen to huge blue saucers of excitement. Our pilot turns to check our seat belts and give us a brief safety drill before his face broadens to a grin as he adds that the sun is hot and the surf is up out on the islands today.

Familiar though this feels, we are not heading home to our Orkney island. Instead this half hour flight is covering the 90km between Auckland City and Great Barrier Island in New Zealand. Rugged, sparsely populated, New Zealand as it used to be, remote, wildly beautiful: we have read so many superlatives about this island that, as island addicts, we just have to go and see it.

On the map this island is comparable to ours - some 30km long and 10km wide. In reality it could not be more of a contrast. We fly in over densely afforested mountains the highest of which, Mount Hobson, peaks at 627Metres. Below us unfold steep gorges, bush streams, switchback dirt tracks and rocky headlands. And then, as we drop into Claris airfield, the splendour of the east coast surf beaches - considered to be among New Zealand's finest - stretch before us.

Within the hour I am lying on the warm sands of Medlands Beach watching that admirable surf hurl Nic and the boys up onto the sand on their boogie boards. Despite the discrete row of bachs (wooden beach houses) set back from the dunes, we have the beach entirely to ourselves and this place feels pretty remote. Just over 1000 people live here without mains electricity or water. Their pace of life is governed by the weather. Every house has its own solar panel or windmill and rain water collecting system.

The untamed feel to this land belies Great Barrier Island's long and busy human history. From a 1,000 years back there was a strong Mauri population interrupted only by the intrusion of European pioneers who tragically raped the land of its majestic Kauri trees and its gold, silver and copper and the surrounding ocean of its whale population. As some small recompense the trees are now regenerating under the protection of the conservation status of some 60% of the island.

Unlike mainland New Zealand, GBI is still free of the imported pest species like possums, stoats, ferrets, deer, Norway rats and hedgehogs. It provides a much needed stronghold for the ground nesting native endangered species such as brown teal, dotterel, banded rail and kaka (parrots). New Zealand's smaller islands are her Noah's Ark.

Toned muscles, pounding heart, adrenalin coursing through our veins - the powerful sea has done what no gym workout could. Miles has broken all records by boogie boarding for 6 continuous hours. Nic, our surf tutor, has re-lived another pastime of his misspent youth. I have found my favourite sea urchin - the sand dollar - in plentiful supply through the sands.

A bird-sized butterfly flutters over the heads of Dale and Fenning as they focus on digging their sand castle moat. Naked but for the grains of sand clinging to their sun bronzed, salt-wet bodies, they're happy as sandboys.

~

Who switched the lights on? We have travelled back through the constant night-time warp of a thirty hour jumbo jet flight from New Zealand to Scotland, Southern Hemisphere to Northern Hemisphere, one end of the world to the other. We have emerged from the fifth and final homeward flight into a blaze of endless daylight that is the Orkney spring. How can we sort our jet-lagged muddle of day from night when it never seems to get dark here?

In fact our sunset was at 8.37pm last night and sunrise this morning was at 3.40am. Add a full moon and clear skies into the equation and you can understand why darkness evades us. A few days ago we were living in a New Zealand autumn – sunrise 7.12am, sunset 5.20pm. A mere ten hours of daylight as opposed to Orkney's seventeen. By next month the sun will only briefly dip below the horizon and our midsummer nights will be lighter than a winter's day. These summer twilights are known here as the "simmer dim" and are celebrated with midnight picnics, rounds of golf and some extra hours of farm work.

The other significant difference is, unfortunately, the temperature. At a latitude of 59 degrees north, Orkney cannot lay claim to a particularly warm climate. As I huddle into my winter woolies once more (Orkney air temperature 7 degrees centigrade aided and abetted by a sharp north-easterly wind) I think back wistfully to our carefree existence of minimal clothing and regular dips in the warm sea (Auckland air temperature 20-25 degrees centigrade).

Climate aside, it's great to be home. One of the first places I visit is my garden. Through bleary eyes I can see that the fuscia and willow hedging is heavily in bud, the herbaceous border plants are beginning to bloom and the lawn is a shag pile of grasses. Through in the veggie plot my tatties and onions are thriving alongside a disappointing plethora of weeds. All my digging and clearing in the weeks before we left has not stopped the weed brigade. I shall have to get gardening again soon...just as soon as I've caught up on some sleep.

Out in the fields nine of our ewes are proudly displaying twin lambs. By far the cutest are the four black ones borne of our Jacob sheep. Our horse, Chuck, has on his fine strawberry roan summer coat and a bit of a rotund grass belly. He and I are overdue for some cantering along the beaches. Omelette the cat comes to purr at my feet. She has clearly had more kittens but she's not ready to show them off yet. We will get to see them in a week or so.

The hen field, where we are planning to create a wee football pitch, is an unruly mess of thistles, dandelions and docken. A long day of strimming looms.

There's lots to do at our island homestead. But for now all I can manage is to pin extra heavy blackout material across our bedroom windows and try to get some sleep.

~

Dead Whale
~ May

At the top of the sand dune I stop short. Laid out on the beach below is a phenomenon the like of which I haven't seen for seven years. A massive sperm whale lies, as if sleeping, parallel to the shoreline. My dog cannot visually comprehend anything on this scale, but she can recognise the smell of death. She whines and cowers in the long dune grasses.

Down on the sands I draw level with this huge sea mammal. I walk heel to toe along the length of the grey, white and pink hulk and count to fifty-two. That's about 50ft, blunt snout to fluked tail. Walking round to the seaward side of the body I can see that he is very obviously male. His tail is ripped and his jaws have been barbarically sawn off. Of course all the teeth are gone. I don't understand the human need for such trophies of the innocent dead.

Standing downwind of his enormous head, the smell of putrefying flesh finally hits my nostrils. The last dead sperm whale I came across was three miles from our home on the Hebridean island of Islay. From memory, he washed up in March and took all summer to decompose. This one washed up six weeks ago and as yet shows little outward sign of rotting. The rather morbid explanation for this is that beached whales overheat and cook themselves from the inside out. Enough said.

Whales are no strangers to Orkney waters. Nineteen different species have been recorded as seen here. The regulars are Pilot (or Caain'), Fin and Minke whales. Blue, Humpback and Right whales also used to pass through Orkney seas until they were hunted to virtual extinction by the whaling industry. A more sustainable way of harvesting whales was employed by most Orcadians as they traditionally only used the blubber from stranded animals. Strandings, however, were not always accidental. At the sight of whales in any Orkney bay the local community would abandon their fields and set out in boats to surround the unfortunate animals and drive them ashore. There they would be killed with anything from a hayfork to a gun by everyone from the humble cottar to the rich landlord. Whale chasing was considered a great sport for the whole community and the profits from the resultant whale oil were divided among all who took part.

Sperm whales tend to stay in the warmer equatorial oceans of the world but lone males of the species do travel north to our waters. They come here to feed on squid in the deep cold waters off our continental shelf. A notable exception to this occurred back in 1976 when a pod of seven females with young came into Scapa Flow. Sperm whales found dead on our beaches are more likely to have died out at sea of illness or old age and then been washed ashore than suffered any more violent ending. Again there are exceptions. In 1994 eleven of these sea giants stranded themselves on Backaskaill Beach in Sanday. Although alive when they beached they died within a few hours as, unsupported by water, their vital organs were crushed by the shear weight of their own huge bodies. Any rescue attempt for such massive and immobile animals was futile and the only sorry task for the islanders (who no longer relish boiling the blubber for oil) was to find somewhere to bury the carcasses. With a cemetery and an archeological site taking up much of the landward side of the bay, this was tricky.

The previous year six male sperm whales swam into Scapa Flow. After several weeks it became obvious that the whales were stuck in the bay and in danger of starvation and locals decided to help them find their way out. Operation "Gentle Shepherd" involved a lot of boats rounding up and pushing this reluctant flock out through the narrow channel which leads to open seas. A poetic reversal of the old whale chasing methods. Five years ago another group of seven whales stayed in the Flow for three weeks before managing to find their own way out.

I realise I've been standing here in a dwam. The fine warm rain has soaked through my jumper. I hate to leave this sleeping giant but it's time to go home.

~

Simmer Dim

~ Summer
2003

Eclipse
~ *June*

I lie awake at 3.30am (with a sunrise of 3.11am and no decent curtains this isn't difficult). I'm looking at an overcast sky and praying that it clears by 4.45am. That's when everyone north of Glasgow should be out looking for the predicted annular eclipse of the sun.

Billed as one of the best places to watch this astronomical phenomenon, Orkney has been filling up with hundreds of stellar enthusiasts over the past week. As the setting moon moves in front of the rising sun we will be cast into shadow and will see a bright ring of sunlight around the blocking moon.

Because such brilliance can damage our eyes to the point of blindness, we should only observe the sun through solar filtered telescopes. In the absence of such equipment, we are relying on the old standby pin-hole camera (of the cereal packet and grease-proof paper variety) technique.

What is known as the moon's "antumbral shadow" – i.e. the twilight zone caused by this juxtaposition of moon and sun – follows a "path of annularity" through north Scotland. By 04.51am it will have passed over our Orkney Island and reached the Faroe Islands. Any Icelandic boat crews out at 05.08am will witness the most dramatic moment of the eclipse before it whizzes across the Denmark Strait and on over Greenland.

Our moon has been up to all sorts this month. Two weeks ago it was hiding behind Earth in a Lunar eclipse. With earth in the way the moon cannot reflect direct sunlight (which is what normally makes it look so white) but only incident light refracted through the Earth's atmosphere. So the moon takes on the colours – reds, browns and oranges – of light that has travelled through dust and cloud. Unfortunately in our case the whole show was obscured by cloud. Better luck later in the month, said the enthusiasts.

So back to this morning's much anticipated eclipse. We're up at 4.30am. Both moon and sun are hiding behind a solid mass of milky-white cloud. We go out anyway, in the hope that we will at the very least detect a darkening of the sky at the appropriate moment. A brisk easterly cuts through our fleecies and has us crouching below the stone dyke for shelter. Curlews, lapwings and several drumming snipe provide an uplifting dawn chorus.

By 5am we are frozen to the bone and have detected absolutely no change in the skies. We resort to a cup of tea and scan of the live internet coverage of the eclipse. The best pictures we can find, damn it, are from an observatory in Belgium.

While moon and sun play hide and seek with us the hundreds of eclipse hunters to visit Orkney must surely be hugely disappointed with this anti-climax. But I hear that at the main venue for viewing the eclipse (Deerness on Orkney Mainland) the locals have wisely laid on live fiddle and bagpipe music and set up a beer tent. Who knows what heavenly spectacle will have been seen from there.

~

Picnic
~ June

We're hot and sweaty and sunburnt. Muscles we had forgotten existed are complaining. Our cheeks are flushed with exertion, limbs livid with thorn scratches and nettle rash. Since 9am we've been digging, strimming, mowing, raking and hoeing. Now it's 3pm and the garden, hitherto wild and straggly, is looking pleasingly tamed and groomed.

Dale requested a beach trip after school today. With ten minutes to bus time I discard my soily boots, scrub my hands and throw together a very rudimentary picnic. We load Wizard (that's the new Landrover's name: green, whizzes along compared to our old one, magic) with wetsuits, towels, picnic and dog (no longer a risky combination, Swan is all grown up now and too polite to touch a picnic uninvited). Dale and Fenning are waiting for us at the road end: their wee red school bus has delivered them and gone.

Out at Cata Sands the tide is high but we can just about keep our wheels dry by driving round the extreme edge of the bay. Swan runs ahead along the stony tide line, darting in and out of the sea grasses to follow the myriad scent-trails of long-gone rabbits. Fulmars flop off their nest ledges at her approach, feigning injury in their attempt to distract her from their chicks.

By common consent we demolish the picnic first. Then the boys repeatedly roll and tumble down the sand dunes removing clothes as they fill with sand until they are entirely naked. Swan leaps up and down with them, wanting to play but mostly getting in the way. We lie on the sand slope in a hollow sheltered from the sea breezes. Warm sunshine soaks through to ease my tired muscles. There's a serene silence and sense of calm, only broken by the boys' laughter. I could easily doze....

Suddenly it's 5.30pm and the day is cooling. It's now or never if we are to jump into the sea. I'm feeling a bit tired and chilly for such an escapade but the boys are all up for it. The great thing about wetsuits is that by the time you have struggled into them you have worked up quite a sweat and the freezing ocean takes on a fresh allure.

We opt for the speed entry method – we all climb the biggest dune then set off at a run for the full impact of diving into the icy waves. Argh! My brain contracts with the shock of cold. A passing seal bobs up within five yards of us, intrigued by these weird intruders into her ocean.

Miles is away on a class trip to Birsay Outdoor Centre on Orkney Mainland this week. For island kids, whose school classes are very small (Miles has one other boy and six girls in his) these trips are a great opportunity to meet up with a few more people of their own age. The trip also involves boats and buses, nights away from home and a chance to get to Kirkwall's joke shop and bowling alley. Wicked.

As the list of activities they are to undertake includes canoeing and raft building I have to assume that he'll be up to his neck in icy waters too. I wish I'd persuaded him to pack his wetsuit.

~

Emergency Services
~ *June*

How many kids can claim to have been airlifted from school (or the field opposite at any rate) to a hospital on another island? One of the school boys here ended up in the air ambulance last week after a playground incident involving some over enthusiastic high jinx on a flying fox.

When an accident requires more than the school secretary's ministrations with antiseptic wipes and plasters, the first person to be called out is the island doctor. Out of surgery hours the most obvious place to look for him is the golf course where he will be doing his best to complete a round without disturbing the nesting mallimak (fulmars) or whaup (curlews), getting attacked in the hard hat area of Skua Alley or falling prey to the cunningly landscaped rabbit warrens.

Our doctor is a wizard at patching and stitching people up, but if there's a suspicion of a broken bone then a flight to Kirkwall's x-ray machine is necessary. And if it's too misty to fly? Then it's over to the services of the RNLI lifeboat for a sea crossing to hospital. Either way it's probably a pretty painful ride with a broken bone.

Mind you, I was once airlifted off the Hebridean island of Tiree when I was eight months pregnant. My 14 stone bulk was crammed into the four seater plane (that was one for the pilot, one for the medic and two for me) on a balmy August evening.

We flew into an azure, blood streaked, dusky sky and with 360 degree views I could see Tiree and Coll, then Iona and Mull, Colonsay and Oronsay and the remote north end of Jura laid out below us in a diamante sea. I almost forgot my pain with the beauty of it all.

Pain, however, is my abiding memory of the subsequent ambulance ride through the streets of Glasgow. All those pot-holes and half finished roadworks were a killer.

The Orkney Island emergency services seem to me to be very efficient and impressively versatile. In addition to their sterling work dealing with boat incidents, the coastguards often have to deal with car accidents – with so many coastal roads it's easy to end up in the sea. Driving off piers is a popular mishap (especially when they are near pubs).

Last year a visitor got disorientated on our single track roads and phoned the coastguard in a panic when he thought his car was hanging off a cliff. He had, in fact, driven into the island's stone quarry (it was a dark, dark night...).

Each of the smaller islands has an auxiliary fire brigade and ours has a peedie (half size) fire engine with a group of local farmers, fishermen and mechanics as her crew. Fire incidents seem happily rare, although there was a nasty one a while back when a campervan blew up and was completely destroyed.

The fire crew attend regular training sessions: only yesterday I saw them out with their engine, apparently dousing the cricket pitch and followed closely by a roller. There's a big cricket match coming up this weekend – Stromness v. Sanday for the Embers Cup – and the pitch obviously needs some emergency treatment.

~

North Isles Sports
~ *June*

Picture this. It's the 20th of June: one day short of midsummer. We're standing on the 30 metre high plateau of a one kilometre wide isthmus of land. Steep, grassy braes to east and west lead down to pale-sand beaches. To our north and south broader stretches of land unfurl. Blashy, gowsterie, cauld wather (cold, sleety showers and blustering winds) chill our bones.

This is a bit late for the Beltan tirls (the May storms regularly experienced in Orkney) but we have had such a dry spring that it's time for a bit of rain. Up here on Sanday they call these storms the Coo-quake (pronounced quack), because they make the kye freshly out from their cosy byres shiver with the cauld wind.

Rain soaks through to our goosebumped flesh. Yet resolute we stand, backs to the wind, collars up, children tucked in front of adults for that peedie smidgen of shelter. And we are not alone in our choice of venue for a day out. We are flanked by some hundred other huddled, shouting, cheering figures. For this is the annual North Isles Sports day, hosted this year by the small and windswept island of Stronsay. What madness made them create their playing fields on the highest and therefore most exposed place on their island I really cannot say, but to give them the benefit of the doubt, it must command fine 360 degree views on a clear day.

Mid-morning saw the arrival of the visiting teams and their supporters. First to sail in through the narrow channel of Papa Sound to Stronsay's picturesque fishing port of Whitehall was the MV Varagen (the vagabond) carrying us from Sanday. Close behind us came MV Earl Siguird fresh from Eday and outside the bay MV Earl Thorfinn waited patiently for space at the pier after her sailing from

Westray. It's not often that we see all three of our North Isles ferry service vessels together.

After a hospitable welcome of soup and homebaking in the community hall, our hosts announce the commencement of battle. 100, 200, 400 and 1500 metre races are valiantly run, with the wind as an extra opponent. Long jump, high jump and shot putt contestants brave the elements. Javelin and discus throwing are not – for obvious reasons – part of the day's events. Who knows where a javelin would fly to with these winds. In the team sports footballs and netballs take on a life of their own, curving and spinning in the westerlies and occasionally flying off on a gust, over the fence and down the brae.

To finish the day there's the traditional tug o' war. Stronsay puts up an impressive team with the help of several Zimarri (beautiful, all encompassing black wool cloaks) clad monks from the monastery on the neighbouring island of Papa Stronsay. But after a hernia inducing struggle it's the burly farmers of Westray who win this battle of brawn.

More tea and cakes and a rather hurried distributing of trophies then we all head for our ferries and dream of the hot baths and roaring fires of home.

~

St. Magnus
~ July

My feel-good factor is sky high. I'm driving the single track, sea-level road that hugs Otterswick Bay. Summer hues of blue, green and yellow fill my field of vision. I salute to three seals sun-basking on the rocks, the shallow waters of the bay sparkling beyond their dark forms. Forage harvesters trundle up and down the green/yellow striped silage fields, sooking up and chopping the cut grass before blowing it into their accompanying silage cart. Terry Wogan has offered up a Beach Boys song to match the moment.

At the War Memorial I turn left into Lady Village. A couple of school kids scoot past on bikes. I laugh at the newly erected speed limit signs. It's hard to imagine going over 40mph through our two villages (especially Kettletoft, which ends with a pier) and I have certainly never achieved the national speed limit on any of our island's narrow, ditch-sided roads.

I'm on my way out to Newark Farm for my weekly fiddle lesson. After six months of no lessons and woefully little attention to my dusty fiddle, I have begun again with a new teacher and renewed determination. Inspiration has come in the form of the "St Magnus Festival on Tour" which this year has provided us with a wind ensemble from the BBC Philharmonic Orchestra. To have such visitors to our tiny island is a great honour - and well worth the adrenaline-driven weekend I spent sweating over Vivaldi's "La tempesta di mare" in F major before we played it with them in concert on Monday.

St Magnus Festival is a world-renowned annual music event and one of the highlights of Orkney's artistic calendar. It all began back in 1970 when a young composer called Peter Maxwell Davies (now Sir Peter) went on holiday to the Orkney island of Hoy. There, in the idyllically remote grandeur of Rackwick Bay, he met Orcadian writer George Mackay Brown. They got on so well that "Max" stayed on and in the end he moved to Hoy and has lived in Orkney ever since.

When he was commissioned to write a piece to commemorate the Queen's Silver Jubilee in 1977, he wrote his opera "The Martyrdom of St Magnus" based on George Mackay Brown's novel "Magnus". It was premiered in 1977 in Kirkwall's magnificent St Magnus Cathedral. The resultant annual festival has grown from strength to strength, with the constant inspirational presence of Max himself as its backbone.

Orkney Mainland of course hosts the lion's share of the festival events. But musicians do hive off to play in the community halls of the smaller islands. The four musicians touring to Sanday this year arrived off Monday's midday boat with their instruments (an oboe, a flute, a clarinet and a bassoon) and were whisked up to the school.

With barely time to draw breath or whet their lips, they taught the recorder group, played for and chatted to all the school kids, rehearsed with us fiddle clubbers and performed an evening concert. Tuesday morning saw them on the boat back to Mainland. Many thanks for fitting us in to their hectic schedule.

~

Retreat
~ *July*

Nic and I are on retreat. You may think that we lead a quiet enough life on this small Orkney island. After all there are less than 600 people sharing it with us and we rarely cross paths with more than a handful of them. We consider it "rush hour" if we meet more than three cars on the five mile road between home and the grocery stores. We can quite happily go for days on end without speaking to anyone but each other and the kids, dog, cats, hens and horse. But just for one weekend we wanted to be sure of freedom from both cars and people. We wanted to look upon a landscape devoid of the materialistic trappings of modern human habitation. We wanted to experience complete silence.

My delightful new mother-in-law (and I write that without so much as a whiff of irony) has offered to hold the fort back home. Even as we leave she is instigating a tough regime of Monopoly, Scrabble, scrubbing behind the ears and early bedtimes. The boys are bemused but happy with these routines and say their farewells to us with a tad too much eagerness for my liking.

After extensive map scanning and a few phone calls we think we have found just the place. A generous farmer has lent us the only habitable cottage on this stretch of his land. It has no electricity or running water but there is a coal-fired stove, a gas cooker and a natural spring of fresh water just down the hillside. We have no need of lighting: at 11pm it's still possible to read if you sit outside.

From the door-stoop of our delightful, wood-lined and anciently wallpapered cottage we can contemplate this green and pleasant land all around us. Our neighbours are sheep and birds. Great black-backed gulls, herring gulls, arctic skuas, bonxies, oystercatchers, redshank, curlew and snipe. Out on the seas surrounding us are those seabirds who prefer not to venture onto land - tysties, guillemots, gannets, shags. We are on another island, of course: how else could we guarantee solitude. I dare not write its name, for fear that when we next go there its peace will have been shattered.

Suffice to say that it took a whole day and some interesting modes of transport to get here. Plane, taxi, ferry, fishing boat, dinghy and, finally standing in a trailer behind a quad bike. We arrive at our cottage wet from the dinghy and splattered with sheep shit thrown up from the quad bike wheels, but exhilarated beyond comprehension. The farmer wishes us well with a wink and zooms off down the hill to his waiting boat, his collie balancing nonchalantly behind him on the quad bike.

Our weekend consists of walking the hills and shores, discovering a wealth of flotsam and jetsam (there's no one else here to search the tide line for treasures) and absorbing the delicious silence. Nic remembers that Billy Connelly didn't realise he had tinnitis until he went to the Antarctic – he had never before been in a quiet enough place to notice.

Our diet is extravagantly odd: we have brought nothing but filet steak, smoked salmon, oatcakes, wine and whiskey (all but the wine are the fine produce of Orkney). For our Saturday night entertainment we set the world to rights over an amber bottle of 25-year-old malt.

By Sunday I'm playing my fiddle to some passing yachts (how dare they enter our personal space!) and we're singing harmonies to the seals. We are beginning to find the cackling gulls and scolding oystercatchers too noisy. Perhaps we ought to go home, before we become total reclusives.

Weather Station
~ July

It's a funny thing, perception. Over many years of island life I have blamed Murphy's Law for the fact that whenever we have visitors the weather seems to turn nasty on us. But I'm beginning to suspect that perhaps our perception of good weather differs from that of "folk frae sooth".

For the most part I find the climate here excellent – plenty of everything and never a dull moment. We get lots of sunshine. I'd like to bet that on Sanday we could match the Hebridean island of Tiree's claim to the highest sunshine hours in Britain. It's just that no one measures it here.

We get an annual rainfall that keeps the farmers happy, yet doesn't impinge on our outdoor lifestyle too badly (and as I keep telling the boys, it's refreshing cycling in the rain). From our small flat island we can watch the rain clouds race, unimpeded, over us and away to more mountainous lands. Many moons ago I lived on Mull, where iron grey clouds could cling to Ben More and envelope us in a damp gloom for days on end.

Wind (of the climatic variety) is an island speciality and I'll admit you have to enjoy being buffeted by some brisk breezes to live here. A neighbour says she relishes our very occasional calm days, but for me these are disturbingly eery and somewhat depressing, like being in the Doldrums, becalmed at sea.

So how come our summer visitors are swathed in fleecie hats and jumpers while we hang out in tee-shirts and shorts? Nic provided the key clue when he returned from a trip to Yorkshire last week saying he'd been sweltering in the heat down there. Aha. After living here for a year he's acclimatised to Orkney temperatures. He also returned with his response to my vague meanderings about the

climate – a high tech 21st century, all singing all dancing, weather station. With Dale helping, he spent most of yesterday rigging the whole thing up and finding a spot for it away from buildings (out in the hen field – lets hope they don't get broody in the rain gauge).

The kit consists of a baro-thermo-hygrometer, a thermo-hygrometer, an anemometer and a rain gauge. The first measures atmospheric pressure, temperature and humidity from within the shelter of the house. The rest measure respectively outdoor temperature, humidity, wind speed and direction and rainfall (even Orkney's horizontal variety). All this information gets transmitted onto a digital display board, which is now the centre of attention on our kitchen table.

At the top is a wee picture of sunshine or clouds, depending, and a barometric scale. By consulting this rudimentary forecast system plus the percentage humidity (or even the dew point, which us washerwomen can use assess the drooth) I can decide whether or not to hang out the laundry. There's even an alarm system that you can set to go off when the temperatures drop to near freezing (get the pot plants in) or the atmospheric pressure drops (cancel the picnic). A memory facility means we can calculate daily, monthly or annual totals or averages.

To my dismay the only thing it doesn't measure is annual sunshine hours. I still can't challenge Tiree's claim.

~

The height of summer and Orkney is in full bloom. Vibrant colours adorn our island like precious jewels scattered on a grass green carpet.

A prolifent display of dark purple and pale mauve orchids (known as Adam and Eve to Orcadians) along verges and through fields is perhaps the most surprising find for newcomers to Orkney. Damp meadows become a swathe of bright pink ragged robin and deep yellow marsh marigolds. Wet channels are lined with elegant stands of yellow iris, while horsetail and marestail whorl through the shallow waters at their feet. Drier fringes of land carpet themselves in dusty yellow bedstraws and peeping eyebrights. Red, white and pink campions flourish along fertile cultivated field edges.

Down on the coast marram, sand couch and sea lyme grasses effectively anchor and bind the sand dunes and allow for a spectacular bloom of flowering species. Pale lilac shades of sea-rocket mix with reddish stalks of spear-leaved orache and the musky fragrance of barely pink sea-stock. Blue-purple flowers of the oyster plant hug the strand lines – sink your teeth into the fleshy green leaves and your mouth will fill with the taste of oysters.

Seaside daisies (sea mayweed) vie with the yellowish green flowers of sea-sandwort for prettiness. Baby pink thrifts share impossibly tiny rock spaces with the spikes of sea arrow grasses and plantains. These last were known as soldiers by Orkney kids who used them in battles, one stalk bashed against its opponent until the flower head fell off.

My sister and her family make the journey from Edinburgh to visit us and see this far-flung be-jewelled island about which I have been waxing lyrical for nearly two years. They stay in a gorgeous old stone cottage along the sand track to Start Point lighthouse. I catch myself thinking I'd like a week there myself, but I guess it's a wee bit daft taking a holiday cottage only a few miles from home.

With their bikes they cycle the length and breadth of the island, take picnics to beaches, breathe the clean, flower-scented air and gradually unwind from their work-stressed lives back in Auld Reekie. On their final day here they try to extend their stay but the ferries are all booked up. Orkney is a popular destination this summer.

I'm driving home with yet another visitor fresh off the boat when I screech to a halt in dismay. The verges have been mown: our orchid strewn roadsides have been cropped short, all the flowers cut down in their prime. But worse: one of our only roadside hedges has been hacked through with a brush cutter. A glorious mix of mature willow, dog rose, hebe, fuschia and birch has been denuded in the midst of its summer flowering.

My consolation comes later in the evening when on a walk through a fabulous area of coastal marshland I come across the shy and unassuming beauty of Grass of Parnassus. Her rosette of five milk-white petals defined by fine green veins lifts my heart.

~

School Holidays
~ *July*

For Orkney kids the six weeks of school summer holidays aren't the long lazy days of my memories. On the contrary the children here have a continuous supply of organized activities to keep them busy. There's no chance to hang around on street corners (even if we had any).

As soon as school broke up, at the end of June, we had a week of Fiddle Club Summer School. Hard on its heels has come three weeks packed with a complex timetable of the following activities.

Week One = "sporty week": football, rugby, roller-skating, table tennis, hockey, basketball, volleyball, rounders, cricket and trampolining.
Week Two = "outdoorsy week": open canoeing, archery, orienteering, pool and sea kayaking, raft building and kite-making.
Week Three = "arty week": fencing, beach trips, bird and wildlife walks, bird-life drawing, felt making and cake decorating.

All this is instigated by a few of our seemingly tireless school staff. Before school broke up they gave every child between Primary Four and Secondary Three the chance to sign up for any or all of the activities. An impressive 95% of our school kids within the right age group decided to take part.

Qualified instruction for these activities comes from several sources. Staff from the Pickaquoy Sports Centre in Kirkwall travel out to the smaller islands to teach the range of sports. Outdoor Education staff also tour the islands with their trailer full of canoes and kayaks for the outdoorsy stuff. Week three encompasses a mix of more artistic disciplines taught by a range of individual experts from all over Orkney.

Having collated the kids' choices, timetabled the events and organized the instructors and venues, our school teachers are finally allowed to go on their own holidays – albeit only as far as their respective farmyards to catch up on the sheep clipping and hay gathering.

Finance for these events comes partly through the ever-pressed School Fund and a nominal fee (£1 per day per family) and partly via a grant from the New Opportunities Fund, which is now in its third and final year. For all of the island kids it is a chance to learn new skills and get fitter, more coordinated and gain confidence.

As a parent of one boy who raves about all the activities (even as I write he is decorating a birthday cake for me) and two boys who can't wait to be old enough to take part, I'm really hoping that some new funding can be found to keep this invaluable programme on the future summer menu.

Now it's the end of July and surely we can squeeze in a quick trip South? Not quite yet – the annual Agricultural Show takes place here at the beginning of August. Having missed it for the past two summers, I'm determined to be here for it this year.

~

Show Day Morning
~ *August*

Show day dawns overcast with a hint of rain. I'm still tucked up in bed but I can imagine the last minute preparations going on all over the island. Brushing and buffing of cattle, an oily rag to stroke a shine onto the black brows of sheep, combing and plaiting of ponies' manes and tails, smart red bandages round their legs. Dogs suffering the discomfort of a shampoo and blow dry. Indignant cockerels temporarily imprisoned in cages and boxes.

At 10am the scene at the showground (the school athletics field transformed) is industrious. Tractors and trailers trundle across the field. Sheep pens fill with the pride of farmers' flocks. The northern perimeter fence is lined with rope-haltered cows, pawing at their ration of hay and nosing their neighbours suspiciously. Along the western fence is the equestrian domain. Bossy ponies aim their rumps and heels at snorting horses. Nets of hay and buckets of water, gleaming saddlery, black boots and hats and jackets. The familiar tar-smell of hoof oil hits me as I walk by.

Judging begins and the roped off ring fills with the first category of in-hand ponies. I refer to my "catalogue of stock". Tixie, Tuppence, Buttons, Star, Mary-Anne and Treacle. That's the mares, next come the geldings – Solstice, Patch, Tango, Noddy and Pippin. Pony names have a classic time-lessness about them.

The sun has struggled out and the rain has stayed away. I wander over to the cattle judging ring. Despite hours of practice back at their farms the cows are reluctant to be led around in a circle and dig their toes in, go down on their knees, buck, attempt a fast exit and bellow their annoyance loudly. Cattle in nearby fields bellow back with contrary emotions – they want to be in on the action. There are bulls, heifers, steers, calves and in-milk or in calf cows. There are Aberdeen Angus, Continental, Black/Blue Polled and Cross-bred cattle.

Round at the sheep pens the Suffolk rams win my top prize for their good looks while their Texel opponents are impressive in their ugliness. Fenning is delighted by the ewes proudly penned with their half-grown lambs and by the patchwork Jacob sheep. The other highlight for the boys is a display of spanking new tractors that they are allowed to climb into and even a toy one that they can ride around in.

The bike shed has taken on a new role for the day as the poultry zone. Cocks crow and leap, hens cluck and ruffle. And along at the end ducks and drakes quack quietly and contemplate their dry feet in bewilderment.

But that's only the half of it. Inside the community hall another aspect of the annual show is on display. The flip side of the coin of rural life. We make our way past the tempting bacon and sausage cooking smells coming from the kitchens and enter the world of domestic Orkney.

~

Show Day Afternoon
~ August

Cabbages fit for Kings, ruby-red beetroots, wax-perfect globes of onions and their baby cousins, shallots. Regiments of carrots, leeks and cucumbers line-up straight and true. Bowls of tomatoes shout scarlet across a table groaning with greens. Saucers of ripe gooseberries tantalise the taste buds. Shafts of sweet purple rhubarb are the emblem of Orkney – it grows so prolifently here.

In the tattie display floury yellows vie with smooth skinned purples with not a black-eye in sight. For every entry there's a plate of cooked tatties alongside, forked open to show off their perfect consistencies. Repeating the pattern, each clutch of hens' eggs is accompanied by one broken open into a dish, golden yolks suspended in diamond clear whites.

Further along the groaning table garden produce gives way to jars of condiments. Jams, chutneys, pickles and curds are produced from the wealth of the Orkney kitchen gardens. All with pretty Sunday bonnets tied around their work-a-day lids.

At the very end of the central table generous platters of chunky meat loaf herald the start of the baking display. In a slightly illogical juxtaposition these wholesome giants are flanked by delicate squares of deep chocolate Tiffin and copiously iced, madly coloured novelty cakes.

Trestle tables run the length of the right hand wall of the community hall for the rest of the extensive range of baking. I can't help a smile at the two foot high chicken wire fence that has been erected between the baking and the viewers.

Fruit-laden clootie dumplings, Victoria sponges oozing jam and cream, fresh buttery pancakes, melt-in-your-mouth oven scones and a variety of specialty breads plaited and rolled to perfection. But for the fence these irresistible goodies would be too much for a hungry onlooker to resist.

Having feasted my eyes I move on round to the arts and crafts along the left hand wall. Items of embroidery, patchwork, knitting and crochet are all beautifully stitched works of art. I especially love the fine white webs of the baby shawls. My babies were all wrapped in these warm cocoons and proceeded to befriend them and drag them through the muddy puddles of toddlerhood as inseparable soulmates. We still have them, manky and matted and a third of their original size but forever loved by their respective owners.

The walls are festooned with photos – a brilliant depiction of island life. Between shots of kids on bikes and dogs on beaches my eye is caught by a close up of an otter eating a fish. Paintings and drawings, clay models, felt collage – the artwork is wide ranging and shows off the wealth of talent within such a small community.

You may be thinking that this insight into domestic Orkney is predominantly the domain of the matriarchs. Not at all. The entries are as likely to belong to men as women. In the children's section boys and girls alike enter decorated cakes, poems in best handwriting, shell patterns in a tray of sand and vase of wild flower arrangements. The best sewn cushion was the work of a fourteen year old boy. His clever stitching depicts the leaping dear motif of a certain well known make of tractor.

~

Lighthouses
~ *August*

It's an ebb tide and my favourite sunny and breezy island weather. Last week I was sweltering in inland Yorkshire. I'm so glad to be back to Orkney and the sea.

We set off on our bikes for a 20 mile round trip across the island. We want to reach the tidal causeway across Ayre Sound well before low tide. This will give us enough time to cross over to Start Island and walk out to Start Point lighthouse and back before the flow tide covers the sound.

All downhill with a following wind and we're through Lady Village and out past Newark before we know it. The dunes around Lopness Bay obscure our view of the sea, so we stop for a breather at the viewpoint and look down on the wreck of the B98, a First World War German destroyer that ran aground here in 1920. Then we're off along the final leg, past the Hearsie Hoose (which houses the old pony-drawn hearse used to carry the deceased back to Lady Kirkyard) and right at Coo Road corner.

In the distance we can see the familiar clown's trouser-leg of our island's lighthouse. The 75 foot conical tower is painted in wide vertical black and white stripes. Minutes later we're off the tarmac and bumping along the sandy track round the south side of the sparkling waters of Scuthvie Bay.

We park our bikes by the boat shed and slip-slide our way across the seaweed strewn rocks, skirting round the deeper rock pools and still sea-filled channels. The Start's grassy track takes us past the sadly derelict farmhouse and across the centre of this beautiful wee island to the formidable buildings of the lighthouse. Erected in 1802, this lighthouse was designed by the first engineer of the Commission of Northern Lights, Thomas Smith,

and his assistant Robert Stevenson (grandfather of the novelist). Robert and his descendants went on to engineer impressive lighthouses all over Scotland. In 1806 Scotland's first revolving light became operational here at Start Point. In 1870 the tower was rebuilt and in 1962 the light was automated.

Out at Tobacco Rock there's a dramatic mix of old-meets-new. Dry stane dykes enclose gardens flourishing with nettles and thistles. Fulmars nest in the derelict cottages and farm byres, roofs sagging and broken with the weight of time. Juxtaposed are the whitewashed lighthouse buildings and a huge bank of solar panels. The powering of lights in these remote spots where reticulated electricity is not an option has made use of oil lamps, diesel generators and gas cylinders before wind and sun began to be employed in the 1990s.

Directly north we have a fine view of North Ronaldsay and with binoculars can get good views of her two lighthouses. There's the old beacon, an astonishingly intact stone tower first lit in 1789. In 1809 the cluster of oil burning lamps that illuminated her were extinguished forever. In the intervening years 22 shipwrecks had occurred: the light was deemed insufficient and the Start Point lighthouse was commissioned. The top of the tower now holds a stone sphere and masonry removed from Start Point in 1806. To her north-west we can see the new lighthouse, a stunning 109 foot red-brick tower lit in 1854 and striped with horizontal white bands. In 1994 the last Orkney lighthouse keeper left North Ronaldsay as it became automated after over 200 years of continuous staffing. The end of an extraordinary era of living in the remotest of places.

Westray
~ August

Throughout the summer season Orkney Ferries puts on a schedule of Sunday excursion trips running between the smaller islands. This means that we can get to our neighbouring islands without first landing on Orkney Mainland. To date I haven't made very good use of these trips – I get caught up in home life and forget to look at the timetable. In this way we have missed out on trips to North Ronaldsay, Eday, Papa Westray and Stronsay.

This Sunday we have managed to organise ourselves for a day trip to Westray. At the civilized hour of 11am the MV Earl Thorfinn rounds the end of Loth pier, ties up alongside and disgorges a few fresh-faced Sanday day trippers. We negotiate the hustle and bustle of hellos and goodbyes, loadings and unloadings, to wheel our bikes on to the vehicle deck and make our way upstairs. The lounge is busy, noisy and stuffy: we opt for the open deck for some fresh air and fine views.

Fine views indeed, from Stany Ayre to Hegglie Ber along Sanday's south-west limb to the castles, caves and geos (rocky sea ravines) of the Middle Old Red sandstone cliff coastline of Eday. We cross today's calm seas where the Eday and Lashy Sounds meet and continue north-west through the narrow confines of Calf Sound. To our starboard lies the Calf of Eday – a generously rounded island of grassy moorland and heathery slopes. I'm surprised that it is uninhabited, with the only house ruins dating back to the Early Iron Age. Has it really not been lived on since?

As well as pre-historic tombs, cairns and houses, The Calf sports the ruins of a 17th century saltworks (the source of most of Orkney's salt between the 17th and 19th centuries) and supports many species of birds. Guillemots, kittiwakes, razorbills and cormorants all nest around the cliffs. Great black-backed gulls are lords of the island, their 1000 strong colony ruling the heathery hill tops.

We slip past Red Head and Grey Head, the northerly sentinels of Calf Sound and out to the open waters of North Sound. The hills of Westray rise high to our port side. Time for coffee and a bacon roll (the finest thing to warm your hands with when out on deck on a chilly ferry trip) before we reach Moclett Pier, Papa Westray. Three cars are hoisted from the boat, swinging precariously in their mesh cradles for a moment before being expertly lowered to rest on the pier. Then we're back out to sea for the final half hour sail to Pierowall.

Westray. Think beef and think fish. These are her main industries. White fish, crab and lobster are all landed at Gill Pier. Multi-coloured piles of fishing nets and towering stacks of creels decorate the two piers enclosing a sheltered harbour busy with trawlers and creel boats. Fishy smells hit our nostrils as we cycle round the bay. At the end of the village we're in for a shock – Westray has steep bits!

After forty minutes of a roller coaster road we're achey limbed and breathless but determined to keep going. We're on a mission to get to a farm down on the southern leg of the island. For today we are collecting Dale's eighth birthday present – a peedie collie puppy.

~

Wrapping Up
~ Autumn
2003

Drooth
~ *September*

I woke this morning to the Radio Orkney newsreader informing us that our summer drooth (drought) is causing water shortages. Our rain gauge has recorded 2.5 inches of rain since we set it up two months ago in July. That's well below Orkney's average summer rainfall, but hardly a drought by, say, African standards. But here on the smaller islands with no riverine system, only a few small lochs and unretentive sandy soils, water supplies can run dry quite quickly.

North Ronaldsay is having to tap into one of its tiny lochs to augment its normal spring water supplies. Shapinsay is being supplied with extra water by way of one or two tanker loads (of 40,000 litre capacity) being shipped to the island every day.

This is to serve Shapinsay's community of 310 people. That's 258 litres per person per day: a figure that I thought astonishingly high until I read that Scottish Water routinely supplies it's 5 million customers across Scotland with 2.5 billion litres per day i.e. 500 litres per head. Our daily use of water supplies is huge: washing machines, flushing loos and the British desire to wallow in deep baths being the main culprits. A lot of water also gets used in the farming industry in a rural community – those cows drink a lot.

Each of the smaller islands of Orkney has its own system for supplying water. Hoy has reservoirs that serve its community and also send water to Flotta and Graemsay via submarine pipes. Eday and Stronsay have bore holes and a new one has just been sunk in Rousay. These are the modern day equivalents of the old wells – reaching down to the water table or aquifers (water saturated rock strata) for a reliable source of water.

At my old house on Islay we shared the cost of drilling a bore hole with the five other families living in our hamlet. The drilling company arrived and doused for water. They "found" it conveniently close to the track up behind the highest house in the hamlet, which also had a big byre good for siting the seven storage tanks. They then drilled down and down. Long into a midge-ridden evening the drilling continued. They were on the point of giving up when, at 210 feet, water was struck. I have always suspected the verity of that dousing.

Here on Sanday our water comes from Bea Loch, a shallow, reed-fringed loch of about 800x600metres in extent. Looking at it on the map, in relation to all the far flung homesteads and farms of Sanday, I find it hard to comprehend that such a small water body can keep us all (about 600 people) supplied, but I am reliably informed that it holds 12.5 million gallons – enough to keep us quenched for a good while.

To treat the Bea Loch water we have some bang up to date technology. In a small shed to the side of the loch is a DAF (dissolved air flotation) and RGF (rapid gravity filters) plant. This high tech treatment filters the water of even the finest of particles, which are harder to remove by sedimentation. Disappointingly, the water still needs to be chlorinated. I loved and still miss the taste of our crystal clear, mineral rich and chlorine-free bore water on Islay. Maybe we should investigate the ancient and beautifully stone-lined well in our back field. Or perhaps not – our septic tank soak-away is only a few yards further up the field.

~

The Orcadian
~ *September*

Thursday is the one day of the week when I try to get down to the village shop. That's the day when Orkney's weekly newspaper "The Orcadian" comes out. I have no need to rush - the paper is delivered by ferry and tends not to reach our shop shelf until afternoon. So here on the islands we read our papers of an evening rather than over morning coffee with the rest of the world.

"The Orcadian" was established by one James Urquhart Anderson in 1854 and is therefore about to celebrate its 150th birthday. But in a sense its history goes back further than that. James' father, Magnus, started the ball rolling by setting up a book binding business in Kirkwall in 1798. A very religious man, his mission was to bind and sell bibles and collections of psalms. Some twenty years later James joined the business and added printing to their skills by way of a small Ruthven Printing Press.

Over the following decades the paper steered through rough seas, almost sinking through bankruptcy several times. At one point opportunist sales of sewing machines and insurance were the only thing keeping "The Orcadian" afloat. But the descendants of Magnus struggled on and by 1931 were able to buy the latest up to the minute technology for a 1930's printing firm - a Cossar Press.

These days the Orcadian has a circulation exceeding 11,000, which ain't bad considering Orkney's total population of 20,000. A copy must find its way onto the majority of Orkney's kitchen tables. Personally I would not want to miss it. My daily dose of Radio Orkney and weekly dose of The Orcadian is what keeps me healthily up to date on all things Orkney. From the small ads ("two cod for sale") to the big news ("proposed international container trans-shipment hub development in

Scapa Flow") the ebb and flow of Orkney life is portrayed.

One of the heaviest books on my shelf ("The Orcadian Book of the 20th Century: a chronicle of our times" by Howard Hazell) is a mega-tome of excerpts from 100 years of "The Orcadian". What I notice when delving into its pages is the prevalence of incidents at sea. Sinkings, drownings, lifeboat rescues, the ups and downs of the fishing industry and of course the years when Scapa Flow bristled with warships. Orkney lives and dies and conquers and thrives by the sea.

Today Nic and I are visiting the print rooms of "The Orcadian" at Hell's Half Acre, Kirkwall. In a modern foyer we admire the huge and beautiful Cossar Press, now in full retirement. On the way to the print rooms we pass floor to ceiling glass casements, the homes of great stacks of leather bound ledgers encasing every issue of The Orcadian from the very first 4 pager printed in 1854.

Through another door we enter the realms of pre-press computers, scanners and image setters. Then come the print rooms busy with an impressive array of modern presses and CMYK printing machines. The three base colours of cyan, magenta and yellow look unlikely to produce a balanced full colour picture. The magenta seems too pink, the cyan too turquoise. But dredge your childhood memories of the primary colours in painting sets and you'll find that they do. Black is the essential fourth ink.

I'm most fascinated by the big rollers and conveyer belts of the newspaper press. But I'm not really here to look at that. I'm here to see a man about a book.

Power
~ September

Up in the north-west of Orkney Mainland there is a windswept moorland called Burgar Hill. Here stand three of the tallest wind turbines I have ever seen. Whenever I drive the lonesome road over that moor I hesitate in the lay-by to watch and listen to them. The graceful arc and deep swish of their powerful blades reminds me of whooper swans flying overhead. They are a fine sight to behold.

I've been put in mind of the windmills by listening to Thursday's edition of "Material World" on Radio Four. To tie in with Orkney's 13th Science Festival the Radio Four team have come up here to look at her renewable energy resources. Wind, tide, waves: these are things we have in abundance here.

Fifty years ago Britain's first big wind turbine was put up by the North Scotland Hydroboard at Costa Head, just up the road from Burgar Hill. Since then wind energy technology has developed disappointingly slowly - through lack of government funding - but it is now a commercially viable power generating system. I'm impressed to hear that the three turbines on Burgar Hill produce 25% of Orkney's electricity requirements. Surely we could find space and capital funding for another nine and be 100% self-sufficient.

Turbines can also be put underwater to harness Orkney's tides. The immense tidal currents of the Pentland Firth and many of the inter-island Sounds are among the most energetic in Europe (no wonder Dale and I are always sick out there). Because water is more dense than air more energy can be extracted from a tidemill than a windmill. It also has a great advantage for folk who worry about countryside aesthetics - there is no visual impact with an underwater turbine. But - despite water wheels having been in use in estuaries for centuries, tidal power technology is not quite ready for the commercial market place yet. Here in Eynhallow Sound, off the coast of Orkney Mainland, a device called a "Snail" is being tested as a way of keeping the tide turbines in position.

Wave energy harnessing devices began with the "Limpet" off the coast of Islay. Then came the "Osprey" near Dounreay and up here we have "Polamis" being tested off the western shores of Stromness. This mechanical sea-snake reminds me of those articulated, painted, wooden snakes which so delight children when you make them weave through the air. It strikes me as a great design for capturing wave energy.

Orcadian attitudes are a fine mix of canny yet innovative, traditional yet open to new ideas. Renewable energy research and development is being embraced here. It's a great opportunity to make use of our fabulous, if sometimes inhospitable, environment. This morning's Radio Orkney news tells me that we are bidding for a European fund being made available for renewable energy research. The bid must come from a team of three island communities each from a different European member state. We are teaming up with Gotland in Sweden and Samso in Denmark. Whether or not we win this bid, Orkney is well and truly in with the renewable energy "in crowd".

Limpets, snails, birds and snakes (and I'm sure I remember a nodding donkey device somewhere in wave power research history). Whatever it takes, why isn't Scotland doing more to harness her wealth of natural power?

~

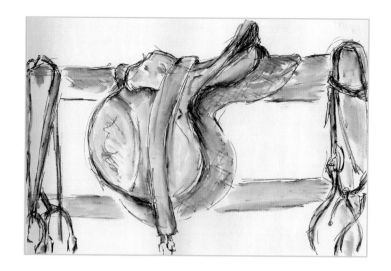

In the news this morning I heard that Scotland's best quality of life is to be found in Orkney. I didn't catch the name of the organisation undertaking the study, but their assertion is based on surveys of health, crime, education and housing in various regions of our country. Their ongoing research programme is now looking at sunshine hours, access to countryside and other environmental factors. Coming to the end of another unprecedently sunny Orkney summer of picnics on deserted beaches I've a feeling we might win on those scores as well.

Last week we had more friends visiting the island. An artist and a photographer, they came on a mission to capture the essence of this paradise in their art. We rented them a cottage by the beach and left them to explore and marvel, bask in the sun, clamber the rocks, walk the shorelines, sketch the wildlife and capture the moonrise on film.

On Saturday we enjoyed a sun drenched day lazing among the sand dunes, jumping in the sea and feasting on a picnic. In the late afternoon Nic took the boys off to the stores to collect the Sunday joint and the weekend papers and comics. With children gone Jess settled with her sketch pad, Jane readjusted her camera after its boy-attack and I lay back in the sand to cuddle Tess, our tired wee puppy. In serene silence the sun dipped below the sand-dunes behind us.

A whisper "what's that?" made me raise my head. Emerging from the sea close to us was an otter. He shook the water from his pelt like a dog then loped up the beach with that unique otter gait before disappearing into the dunes. Otters have acute hearing but are fairly short-sighted. Because of our silence and stillness he hadn't noticed us at all. And we were so breath-taken by this close encounter that none of us thought to grab a camera. It was one of those moments to commit to memory rather than film.

Now it's mid-week. Everyone's gone - visitors and Nic down south, boys at school. I'm out in the yard saddle-soaping Chuck's tack and contemplating life, the universe and everything. Here I am, living an idyllic life on a remote archipelago. We have the space and freedom and fresh air that I sought. The boys can cycle off to see friends without me worrying that they will encounter anything worse than a muddy ditch. We are surrounded by beautiful beaches. Our eyes can focus on distant horizons, unimpeded by buildings. I can breathe the fresh salt air of the sea.

No wonder Orkney rates so highly in society's quest for quality of life. I only hope it doesn't get too popular or I may have to move further north (I've been eyeing up the Faroe Islands recently).

The wind has swung north this week and there's an autumnal chill in the air. It's time to look out the woolly vests, thick socks, hats and gloves. Instinct tells me we're in for a rough winter. After such a warm summer we're due some wild storms to remind us that we live on a set of tiny islands in the middle of a great big cold ocean.

But today the weather is still beautiful. I catch Chuck, brush him down, pick the mud from his hooves and tack him up. The dogs leap with joy and run ahead as I gather up Chuck's reins, reach my left foot into the stirrup and swing up into the saddle. We set off along the grass track to the beach, autumn sun warming our backs, sea sparkling in the distance. Fine That.

~

Orcadian Wirds

I have used a few Orcadian words as I learn them. Most often they are explained within the story. For a comprehensive dictionary see the References but bear in mind that every island (and even within parishes within each island) has its own dialect.

blashy = heavy sleety showers
buddy = person, *man-buddy* = a man, *wife buddy* = a woman
bruck = rubbish
drooth = drought or a drying wind
dwam = daydream, drifting thoughts
fendan = foraging
ferry-loupers = non-natives to Orkney, those who have arrived by ferry
fine that = very good
flittin' = moving
gaan hame = going home
glaamsie skies = forboding skies
gowsterie = windy
hame = home
humph = carry heavy things
kye = cows, *coo* = one cow
maet = food, *ebb-maet* = seafood
peedie = wee, little
simmer dim = light nights of summer, when the sun barely dips below the horizon
skeetan stanes = skimming stones over water
skutherie weet = light, intermittent rain showers
sheed = small field
stabs = stobs, wooden fencing posts
weet = wet
wirds = words

References

Armitage, Don (ed) *Great Barrier Island* Canterbury University Press, NZ 2001

Berry,RJ *Orkney Nature* T&AD Poyser 2000

Bathurst, Bella *The Lighthouse Stevensons* Flamingo, London 2000

Campbell, AC *Seashores & Shallow Seas of Britain & Europe* Hamlyn, London 1989

Carwardine, Mark *Whales, Dolphins & Porpoises* Dorling Kindersley, London 2000

Chapman J C & Mytum H C (eds) *Settlement in North Britain 1000BC-AD1000* 1983

Cobb, John *Explore New Zealand* New Holland Pub. Ltd. Aukland NZ 2001

Fitter, Richard & Alastair *The Wild Flowers of Britain and Northern Europe Collins, London 1980*

Flaws, Margaret & Lamb, Gregor *The Orkney Dictionary* The Orkney Language & Culture Group, Orkney 2001

Garrioch, T. *Aald Wirds used in Sanday*

Haswell-Smith, Hamish *The Scottish Islands* Canongate Books Ltd, Edinburgh 1999

Hazell, Howard *The Orcadian Book of the 20th Century.* The Orcadian Ltd. Orkney 2000

Hewison, W.S. *Scapa Flow in War and Peace* Bellavista Pub. 2000

Hewison, W.S.(ed) *The Diary of Patrick Fea of Stove, Orkney, 1766-96* Tuckwell Press, Scotland 1997

Krauskopf, Sharma *Northern Lighthouses* The Shetland Times Ltd. Lerwick 2003

Meek, Eric *Islands of Birds* RSPB 1985

Thomson, William *The New History of Orkney* Mercat Press, Edinburgh 2001

Thomson, William *Kelp-making in Orkney*

Towsey, Kate (ed) *Orkney and the Sea an oral history* Orkney Heritage 2002

Moonart

The photographs and illustrations for this book are provided by Jane Young and Jess Wallace of Moonart, established in 1999 to provide a range of visual arts for publication and performance.

Through Moonart Jess and Jane have produced work in a variety of media from precise dinosaur fossil drawings for the Natural History Museum, to improvised sets for dance, video for documentaries and photographs for specialist equine publication.

They have a fluid, creative and committed approach to every project.

www.moonart.co.uk